North Carolina Legends

North Carolina Legends

Richard Walser

Drawings by Bill Ballard

Raleigh
Division of Archives and History
North Carolina Department of Cultural Resources
1980

Eighth Printing, 1987

HARD-COVER COPIES ISSUED:

First Printing, 1980 .... 1,000 copies
Second Printing, 1981 .... 1,000 copies
Third Printing, 1984 .... 1,000 copies

PAPERBACK COPIES ISSUED:

First Printing, 1980 .... 3,000 copies
Second Printing, 1981 .... 4,000 copies
Third Printing, 1982 .... 5,000 copies
Fourth Printing, 1982 .... 5,000 copies
Fifth Printing, 1983 .... 5,000 copies
Sixth Printing, 1984 .... 10,000 copies
Seventh Printing, 1986 .... 5,000 copies
Eighth Printing, 1987 .... 10,000 copies

Contents

Foreword

North Carolina is a state whose history has been enriched by legends and folklore. Tales of mystery and the supernatural, stories about the famous and the infamous, well-known sayings that have become intertwined with historical facts—these add color to the pattern of the Tar Heel State's development.

Questions often arise as to the origin of these sayings and tales. Never before have so many legends been brought together as in this latest publication by Richard Walser. Mr. Walser has been writing and editing for nearly five decades, and he is one of North Carolina's best-known authors. The Division of Archives and History previously published his *Young Readers' Picturebook of Tar Heel Authors*; his edition of Lemuel Sawyer's 1824 *Blackbeard*; a history of literature and writers called *Literary North Carolina*; an edition of *The Poems of Governor Thomas Burke of North Carolina*; and several articles in the *North Carolina Historical Review*. Books by Mr. Walser have been published by other presses, including those of the University of North Carolina and Duke University. *North Carolina Legends* will enhance a reputation already established for accuracy of content and for literary quality.

Mrs. Mary Reynolds Peacock, historical publications editor previously on the staff of the Historical Publications Section, was responsible for editing and seeing the publication through the press. Illustrations were produced by Bill Ballard of Raleigh.

Jeffrey J. Crow
Historical Publications Administrator

August 17, 1987

Large Turtle

The little village of *Murphy* ... lies at the junction of the
Owassa and Valley rivers, and in point of location is one of the
prettiest places in the world. Its Indian name was *Klausuna*, or
the *Large Turtle*. It was so called, says a Cherokee legend, on
account of its being the *sunning* place of an immense turtle
which lived in its vicinity in ancient times. The turtle was particularly famous for its *repelling* power, having been known not
to be at all injured by a stroke of lightning. Nothing on earth
had power to annihilate the creature; but, on account of the
many attempts made to take its life, when it was known to be a
harmless and inoffensive creature, it became disgusted with
this world, and burrowed its way into the middle of the earth,
where it now lives in peace. (Charles Lanman)

The Moon-Eyed People

In the long, long ago, before the Cherokee came from their home-land of great snakes and water monsters to the mountains of blue smoke and sparkling streams, so say the Old Men, there lived in these beautiful hills and glades a race of men who were not Indians. These men had white skins, bearded faces, and blue eyes like the sky, and they were here even before the lusty Spaniards who came seeking gold. They possessed all the land from the Little Tennessee River to Kentucky, with a line of fortifications from one end of their domain to the other.

These white men lived in little houses of logs and mud, dug out from the inside, and they never emerged from their rounded dwellings in the daytime because they were blinded by light. They came out only at night, in the dark of the moon, to hunt, fish, build their mounds and fortifications, and carry on warfare. During the full moon they were stone blind, and so they were called the Moon-Eyed People.

Once at the full of the moon, say the Old Men, the cruel Creeks came up from the south and drove the Moon-Eyed People from their beautiful homeland. Whence they came, and whither they went are equal mysteries, but it is told that they were driven far to the west toward the setting sun, and vanished into its light.

There is no proof that such a people ever existed; and there is no valid explanation for the crumbling mounds and fortifications that the Cherokee disclaim, but there are several legends that seek to un-ravel the mystery.

One tale is that the Moon-Eyed People were small folk, perfectly white, who lived at the mouth of Peachtree Creek near Murphy. As they could not cross the creek because the Great Leech who inhabited its waters would swallow them up, they went west in a time before history.

Another story says the Moon-Eyed People were Welshmen who sailed with Prince Madoc about 1170, finally reached this land, and settled in the Great Smokies.

And still another tells of a people, white, bearded, and blind in the light, who lived on Hiwassee, built mounds and fortifications and, for some unknown reason, went west before the coming of the Indians.

Were there really Moon-Eyed People—white, blue-eyed, and bearded—who lived in the Smokies before recorded time? Nobody knows. (Julia Montgomery Street)

Judaculla Rock

On the banks of Caney Fork Creek in Jackson County is a huge soapstone rock, its surface completely covered with strange markings unlike others in the mountains. One of the symbols seems to be that of a large seven-finger hand print.

Legend has it that long before the Cherokee came to the region, the area was inhabited by a slant-eyed giant taller than the pine trees. His name was Judaculla or Tsulkalu, and he was a mighty hunter. When thirsty, he would drink a whole creek dry. When hungry and in pursuit of game, he would jump from one mountain top to another in a single leap. He had a farm on a high peak, and from it he kept watch over his domain.

Once a hunting party of Indians wandered into the valley of Caney Fork Creek. From his mountain lair Judaculla saw them and was angered that a band of puny creatures had penetrated his hunting territory. He gave a mighty roar and sprang down to kill them. On landing in the valley, he stumbled and put out his hand to steady himself. So powerful was his thrust that his seven fingers pressed into the soapstone, and there their imprint can be seen to this day.

Starlight at Blowing Rock

Though the mountain chieftain Osseo governed a vast realm rich in game, his proudest possession was a beautiful daughter known to the tribe as Starlight. At sixteen she was courted by many suitors, but Osseo refused all their offers because she alone of his sons and daughters could sway his savage but noble heart. He did not wish to part with the most beneficent influence on his life.

One day she stood before him. "O chief and father, I pray you appoint some means by which I may wed, for it is not fit that you should wait till I am old and ugly, and you must then beg for suitors for the hand now humbly entreated for."

"Have you grown tired of your maidenhood, my daughter? Do you wish some strange man to rule over you who are so starry-eyed and proud?"

"Father, I yearn for love only, and so great is that yearning that I will sacrifice all for it."

"So be it then."

Messengers went throughout the realm, proclaiming that Starlight would choose a husband from among the braves who came to plead their cause. The day was set. The place chosen was a level ground on the verge of a precipice high above a valley through which wound a sparkling stream. Of the many suitors who came, the bravest and most handsome was Kwasind, and it was he who found favor with Osseo and Starlight. But before she could proclaim her choice, a jealous suitor, stung by his rejection, whispered to Starlight the untruth that Kwasind, in a far-off land, had deserted his bride. Starlight was heart-weary. She loved the well-favored Kwasind, but when he came forward to plead his cause, she said, "Sooner would I see you dead than choose you as my husband."

He turned away. "Then my life is of no value to me," he said. "See how I love you!" Stepping over the narrow barrier of stones, he leaped from the precipice and fell down, down, down. The maiden, wildly penitent, shrieked: "O Strong West Wind, bring my lover back to me! O Sweet South Wind, bear him up in your gentle arms!"

The two brothers, the West Wind and the South Wind, heard her and, moved by her beauty and grief, blew Kwasind back to the spot where Starlight lay sobbing on the stone eminence. He lifted her up, showered kisses on her dark hair, and pressed her to him.

"My lord," whispered Starlight, "forgive me and I will follow you forever to the ends of the earth."

And so it is, even today, that an object cast from the Blowing Rock will be thrown back to the visitor who stands high upon it.

Waccamaw

The largest body of water in southeastern North Carolina is Lake Waccamaw, seven miles long and five miles wide. It is drained by a rambling river, meandering and turning almost upon itself through the swamps till it empties into the Atlantic Ocean sixty-five miles away.

A myth tells of the time when the world was created and the Great Spirit found he had a lot of river he had not used. "I know what I shall do," he said, and so he twisted and curved what was left over, winding it backward and forward across the swamps south of Lake Waccamaw. Nowadays it takes a canoeist many times the direct sixty-five miles to reach the ocean.

The lake itself was once a large expanse of flowers, cared for by a Waccamaw Indian princess known as the Keeper of the Wild Flowers. Each neighboring chief, to ensure happiness and good fortune for his tribe, sent his oldest son to the charming Keeper, and she presented him with a wild rose for good luck.

A young chieftain from the north came to receive his wild rose. So struck was he with the beauty of the princess that he asked her father, the Waccamaw king, for her hand in marriage. But the Great Spirit had ruled that she, as Keeper of the Wild Flowers, would never be allowed to wed. She was to live only to do the work of the Great Spirit. The handsome young prince was enraged. He returned to his tribe, gathered his warriors, and returned to the land of the Waccamaws. All of the Waccamaw braves were killed and the flowers destroyed.

The Keeper of the Wild Flowers had hidden in the swamp. There she pleaded with the Great Spirit to let her die too. She also asked that the flowers not be allowed to bloom again, so that never in the future could man destroy such loveliness. At that moment, the princess dropped to the ground, the land sank, and the waters of Lake Waccamaw appeared.

Prince Madoc the Welshman

In 1170, upon the death of the Welsh king in Great Britain, the succession was contested by several of his ferocious, brutish sons. Twelfth-century Wales was a barbarous country and the most heinous atrocities went unpunished. As the brothers, incited by the king's evil widow, slaughtered each other, the winsome youngest son, whose name was Madoc, decided to leave his bloody homeland. The twenty-year-old prince gathered together more than a hundred of his peace-loving followers and sailed into the unknown western seas, hoping to find an untroubled land where they could live happily and congenially with each other.

He found it. Beyond the ocean was a beautiful, bounteous realm peopled by dark-skinned natives who led industrious, harmonious lives. After a year, leaving behind most of his companions, Madoc went back to Wales for supplies. The report on his new home was ardently received by the strife-weary people, and ten shiploads of his countrymen returned with him into the west. They were never heard of again.

Five centuries later in 1666, Morgan Jones, a Welsh clergyman, sailed south from Virginia. Some weeks after landing at a dismal spot on the coast, he became so beset with hardships that he started an overland trek back north. On the banks of the Pamlico River in North Carolina he was taken captive by a Tuscarora tribe of Doeg Indians, many of whom had fair complexions and red hair. He was condemned to die the next morning.

All night Jones prayed for deliverance, exclaiming over and over again in Cymric, "Have I escaped so many dangers that I must now be knocked on the head like a dog?"

A chief of the Doegs heard him and spoke to him in the same strange but wonderful language. "You speak our tongue," he said. "You shall not die."

For four months Morgan Jones stayed with the Doegs, preaching to them three times a week in Welsh. Finally resuming his journey, he promised to go to Great Britain and come back with missionaries to instruct the tribe in the Christian faith. His death left his mission unaccomplished.

Only much later was it conjectured that the Doegs were descendants of Madoc's Welsh explorers and the blessed natives of the western seas.

Virginia Dare the White Doe

In 1587 Sir Walter Raleigh sent men and women from England to establish a colony in the New World. It was his second attempt, for the first colonists of 1585 had abandoned Roanoke Island after a number of disastrous events. The governor of the second colony, John White, had with him two Indians, Manteo and Wanchese, who had earlier been taken to London. Also in the group was Eleanor Dare, the governor's daughter, and her husband Ananias.

A month after the colony's safe arrival, Virginia Dare was born on August 18. The first English child born in the New World, she was the daughter of Eleanor and Ananias. On August 27, three days after her baptism, Governor White sailed to England for supplies. In England his country was preparing for war with Spain, and for several years he could not get permission to return. When finally he came back, he found no trace of the colonists. Virginia Dare had vanished.

Or had she? There is a legend that she grew into a beautiful young woman, educated by her good friend Manteo in the ways of the forest. She was loved by many but especially by the handsome young Indian chieftain Okisko. When an old witch doctor named Chico turned Virginia into a White Doe because she spurned his protestations of love, Okisko was determined to undo the magic. From a kindly magician he learned that the only way to do so was to pierce her heart with an arrow of oyster shell.

Meanwhile, the evil Wanchese, who hated the English, also had been spurned by Virginia Dare and he was determined to kill the White Doe with a silver arrow given him by Queen Elizabeth while he was in England. Wanchese well knew that a White Doe lives a charmed life and death can come only from a silver arrow.

One day, as Okisko searched along the shore for the White Doe, suddenly there she was, springing from the deep forest down to the white sands where Governor White's fort had once stood. He raised his bow, aimed his arrow, and the pearl arrow sped away. At exactly the same moment, from another direction, a silver arrow came toward the White Doe from the bow of Wanchese. The two arrows pierced the heart of the Doe simultaneously.

The White Doe resumed her form as a beautiful maiden, but she was dying. Wanchese rushed away, and Okisko looked for the last time into the eyes of his beloved Virginia Dare. He sorrowfully buried her in the center of the abandoned fort.

Batts Grave

A hurricane in the 1950s sank an island beneath the surface of Albemarle Sound. A shallow, muddy bottom off the banks of Perquimans County is all that remains of what centuries ago was a beautiful island with fields and trees and orchards and a lone house. During the early days of the colony, in the 1660s, it was owned by Nathaniel Batts, the very first settler to come to North Carolina and remain here. So influential and fearless was he that those settlers who followed him called him "Captain Nathaniel Batts, Governor of Roanoke."

Batts was a "rude, desperate man" who did not like the other white settlers, preferring the Indians of the Chowan tribe. With them he went hunting and trapping, and when they were at war with other tribes, he fought alongside them. Much of the time he lived with the Indians, adopting their customs and dress. It is no wonder that he and the chief's daughter Kickowanna fell in love. She told Batts that when her father died he would become chief of the Chowans, and so she adorned him with gaudy ornaments and a headdress of feathers befitting his future status.

From time to time Batts would retire to his little house on the island he owned, and there Kickowanna would come to visit him, paddling her canoe silently across the waters of Albemarle Sound. Late one afternoon she was on her way to the island when a sudden storm came up, her canoe was overturned, and she was drowned in the roiling waters. Thereafter Batts never left the island. Several years later, it is said, he died of a broken heart and was buried on the island, which then became known as Batts Grave.

On stormy nights, the ghost of Batts sweeps about among the cawing sea gulls, grieving for his lost love Kickowanna.

The Ship of Fire

On a certain evening every year, at the mouth of the wide Neuse River, a large bright object speeds into view. It looks like a sailing ship being destroyed by fire, its deck and masts in blazing outline. The apparition disappears, then reappears, then again disappears for another year. It burns furiously but is not consumed.

It is the ship of the Palatines. The Palatines were a group of German Protestants who left England in 1710 to settle New Bern. As the vessel crossed the Atlantic, the prosperous Palatines, pretending to be poor, hid their gold coins and silver dishes from the eyes of the ship's sinister captain and crew. When the Palatines caught sight of the shore which they believed to be their future home, so excited were they that up from the hold and out from hiding places came all their belongings in preparation for landing. Unwisely displayed on the deck

was their precious wealth, all of it in full view of the corrupt captain and his first mate.

Quickly the captain formed a plan. He announced to the passengers that no landing could be made until the morrow. The disappointed Palatines once more hid their valuables and lay down to a sound sleep in anticipation of soon landing at their destination. When all was quiet, the captain gathered his crew together and revealed to them his plan. They would murder every Palatine aboard—the young and the old, the women and children as well as the men—then gather together the gold and silver, set afire the ship filled with its dead, and escape in the lifeboats.

The strike was sudden. Many Palatines were knifed before they awoke and in a very few moments every one of them was dead. As planned, the ship was set afire, and the murderers pushed off in the small boats. From a distance they looked back at the ship. It burned brighter and brighter, the brilliant blaze of the fire shooting into the air, but the vessel did not sink into the water. And then the thing began to move.

"It continued to burn all night," according to an old account, "—speeding on with the wind,—now passing out from sight, and anon, visible, flaming forever, back again, on the very spot where the crime had been committed. With the dawn of day, it had ceased to burn,—but there it stood, erect as ever, with the spars, sails, masts, unconsumed,—everything in place, but everything blackened, charred." At sundown the flames leaped up again—"a ship on fire that would not burn!"

The frightened murderers could bear no more. They abandoned their boats on the bank of the river and fled into the forest. There they and their descendants lived on their "ill-gotten spoils." To this day the crime has not been avenged, and so every year on a certain evening the burning ship appears off New Bern, and so it will continue to appear till the blood of the Palatines has been paid for in kind.

Blackbeard's Last Fight

Of the many pirates who ravaged the coast of North Carolina during the early years of the eighteenth century, by far the most fearsome was Blackbeard. He had been born in England with a name such as Edward Teach or Thatch or Thach, but because of his grizzly hair the color of midnight, he soon was appropriately nicknamed Blackbeard. Sometimes to make himself even more horrible, he would attach slow-burning fuses to some ragged tuft of his inky beard to give the impression he was about to blow up. Not even heavy-armored men-o'-war awed him, but when the odds became too great, he would

retreat through a shallow North Carolina inlet and hide behind the sandbanks.

Governor Charles Eden was so cowed by this scurvy villain that he let him roam at will along the coast. Tradition says the privateer even gave the governor some of his booty. Most of his treasures the pirate buried at one place or another on the shore. At his house in the town of Bath, Blackbeard settled briefly with his thirteenth wife, but he was restless and soon was back at sea, raiding vessels from Virginia and South Carolina. When Governor Eden couldn't, or wouldn't, do anything to stop him, the governor of Virginia sent Lieutenant Robert Maynard to catch the corsair.

At Ocracoke before daylight on November 22, 1718, they met: Maynard's sloop and Blackbeard's *Adventure*. The two ships touched, and vicious Blackbeard jumped aboard the sloop and faced the lieutenant. Maynard drew blood first with a bullet right through the pirate's body, but the freebooter fought on. Finally, with a mighty swish of his sword, Maynard severed Blackbeard's head from his trunk. The head dropped into the water and circled the ship three times, crying out, "O crow, Cock! O crow, Cock!" The crowing of a cock signaled the coming of morning, and Blackbeard wanted enough light to find his body. But it was too late. Maynard's men counted twenty-five wounds in the pirate. They retrieved the head, swung it to the bowsprit of Maynard's ship, and sailed from the island.

The Birds Weren't Singing

Near Johnsonville, fifteen miles south of Sanford, is a burial mound that is the common grave of more than a hundred Indians. Fragments of bones can still be found there. In the early 1700s, before the Scots settled the area, the surrounding region was the hunting grounds of the Sapona Indians. They warned neighboring tribes to keep away, and for the most part their warning was heeded.

However, after one particularly disastrous hunting season, the Indians down along Drowning Creek were so hard-pressed that they decided to venture into the rich Sapona lands, make a quick foray for game, and return to their homes before the Saponas knew they had been there.

And so they marched north. The signs were ominous. On the evening before their intrusion into the forbidden forests, the smoke of the campfires clung to the ground, and in the distance the wolves howled. One of the braves was alarmed and urged the hunters to turn back. But their need was great, and they moved on. The following morning, as they stepped quietly alongside a huckleberry bog, the alarmed brave stopped in his tracks. Every hunter in the party stopped. There was silence, overwhelming silence, deadly silence.

"The birds," he whispered. "There are no birds singing." And then in a shout, "Run! Run for your lives!"

It was too late. A rain of arrows sped toward them. The sound of war whoops blotted out the silence. The Saponas sprang from behind the huckleberry bushes, their tomahawks raised. In a moment it was all over. The dead intruders were stacked into a shallow pit and covered with dirt.

Only a few survivors escaped and from them the Scots, when they came as settlers to the upper Cape Fear, learned about the massacre.

Troubles in Bath Town

Though Bath was the first town to be established in North Carolina, it is today only a sleepy little village on the Pamlico River in Beaufort County. It wasn't always sleepy. In the first part of the eighteenth century, it was a thriving port, with ships from foreign countries tied up at its docks. Merchants made big money in trade, sailors kept the taverns busy, and the ladies of the town were dressed in the finest clothes. It had a library and a beautiful church. No town in North Carolina could match its prosperity, not even Edenton or New Bern or Wilmington.

Bath's luck was to change. Though in its first decade the pirate Blackbeard corrupted the place by making shady deals with the shopkeepers and even the colony officials, Bath pretended nothing was wrong.

At mid-century, the great evangelist George Whitefield visited the town on several occasions, preaching against cursing and drinking and dancing—especially dancing. To him, dancing was the way the devil sent frivolous men and women to hell. The affluent folk of Bath were suspicious of Whitefield and his fire-and-damnation sermons. For one thing, they didn't like the way the traveling preacher always carried his coffin in his wagon. Whitefield said that if he died, he wanted his coffin right there. The people in Bath thought such a notion was very odd indeed. Furthermore, he slept in the coffin to avoid the bawdy goings-on at the local inn. Though Whitefield kept returning to Bath and attempting to reform it, he finally gave up. On his last trip, he was told he could no longer preach in the town. The discouraged man got into his wagon, took off his shoes, shook them vigorously, and drove off, muttering, "There's a place in the Bible that says if a place won't listen to The Word, you shake the dust of the town off your feet, and the town shall be cursed. I have put a curse on this town for a hundred years."

In truth, the town began to decline. Ships went elsewhere, wealthy merchants moved away, and few newcomers arrived to build houses. A hundred years later the place was hardly worth calling a town. And then something else happened to tarnish Bath's reputation.

A man named Jesse Elliott was a great racehorse enthusiast. At the track near Bath he would take on any challenger, any hour of the day, any day of the week. His chestnut stallion, he believed, was superior to any other horse in the country. One Sunday morning down by the dock in Bath, a stranger on a shiny black horse approached Elliott and said he'd bet a hundred dollars that the stallion could be beaten. "I'll meet you at the track in an hour," said Elliott, who rode off home to prepare for the race. Elliott was a profane man, a whiskey drinker. As he put on his riding boots, he downed two glasses of straight liquor.

His wife warned him not to race on Sunday. Instead of listening to her advice, he lunged at her, cursed her, and beat her to the floor. As he left the house and mounted his stallion, his wife called after him, "I hope you'll be sent to hell this very day."

At the track, the stranger met him. His dark eyes gleamed, and his ears and nose seemed pointed in a way Elliott had not noticed earlier. Terms were agreed upon, and off they shot, Elliott soon in the lead. He shouted to his horse, "Take me in a winner or take me to hell!" The stranger, as he rode behind, appeared not to be disturbed. Suddenly, at a curve in the track, the stallion twisted his head around and shied. Did the horse get a glimpse of the challenger—a terrified glimpse of a reddish figure astride a black horse, his evil mouth wide open in a soundless laugh? In any case, the stallion leaped high on his hind legs, dug his hooves in the soft earth, and threw Elliott against a tree, killing him instantly. The stranger disappeared in a flash.

There are those who say that the soul of Jesse Elliott, in accordance with his wife's curse, went to hell that very moment, taken there by the stranger on the black horse. The stallion dashed into the forest and was never caught. All that remained was the hoofprints, which can be seen to this very day.

Since that awful moment, Bath has slept pleasantly along the river, Whitefield's words have long been forgotten, and only the hoofprints are there to remind visitors to the historic town of some less sleepy times in the past.

Old Dan Tucker

Born in London in 1714, Dan Tucker was brought by his parents to Bath Town in eastern North Carolina six years later. In 1740 he married Margaret DeVane and moved inland to what is today Randolph County, and there near a spring he built his cabin. Since he had no nails, he used wooden pegs to hold the cabin together. This experience proved to him that man could get along very well without many of the things thought to be essential. He became very, very thrifty. He washed his face in a frying pan instead of a bowl, and instead of a comb he used a wagon wheel—or so his neighbors said as they began making up humorous songs about him.

Dan Tucker was kind and honest, ever eager to help his friends, whom he often visited. But never would he accept an invitation to supper, believing that he should provide for himself rather than eating his neighbors' food. Because of this, they began to sing that he always came too late to get his supper.

One morning, while plowing in the field, he stepped on a tiny sharp rock, which became imbedded in his heel. With an unclean pocket knife he cut the stone out and as a result fell victim to lockjaw. A few days later he died "with a toothache in his heel"—as the song puts it.

In spite of his odd and curious ways, Dan Tucker was loved and respected, especially for the square deals he always gave his friends.

Old Dan Tucker was a fine old man;
He washed his face in the frying pan;
On Christmas morning he got drunk
And fell in the fire and kicked up a chunk.
    Get out of the way, Old Dan Tucker;
    You've come too late to get your supper.

Old Dan Tucker ate raw eel
And combed his hair with a wagon wheel.
He gave his neighbors the squarest deal
And died with a toothache in his heel.
    Get out of the way, Old Dan Tucker;
    You've come too late to get your supper.

How Dan'l Boone Nearly Nipped a Romance

Jim Bryan was a good friend of Dan'l Boone's, and his cabin was in a clearing near the forks of the Yadkin. His daughter Rebecca wasn't more than fifteen, and she thought a right smart of Dan'l.

Late one morning Boone came out of the woods into the clearing and yelled Jim out of the cabin. Jim hadn't seen Dan'l for a long time and was mighty glad to see him. After they had some dinner that

Rebecca cooked herself, Dan'l said he might stay in that part of the country for a long time, but Jim didn't believe it.

Jim talked about how the mountain lions were getting so bad, and Dan'l said they ought to go hunting that night. Back then the men hunted mountain lions at night, and carried a big pan of wood coals to make their eyes show up in the dark. All the hunters had to do was shoot between the eyes.

Rebecca liked to hunt too, and after the men left that night, she followed them.

The men had already got six lions, and had started back to another place to hunt when Jim saw two eyes shining over to one side. He yelled, and Dan'l dropped to one knee and fired. There was a loud scream, and the men didn't know what to do. Then they heard some crying over where Dan'l had shot, and they went to investigate.

They found Rebecca behind a tree, and a dead kitten was on the ground beside her. She said she had been holding the cat in her arms and somebody had shot it. She went home crying, and Dan'l followed her to explain that he didn't know it was a cat.

Jim hadn't believed it possible, but Dan'l did stay in that country a long time—about two years, long enough to marry Rebecca. (Anonymous)

Betsy Dowdy's Ride

I n December, 1775, at the outset of the Revolution, Virginia's royal governor, Lord Dunmore, began marching south from his base at Norfolk to subdue the Albemarle Sound area. He needed horses for his soldiers, and he had his mind set on capturing the swift half-wild ponies whose progenitors were an Arabian breed wrecked on the sandbanks many years before. The only force able to stop Dunmore was a small American army under General William Skinner camped over in Perquimans County. Lord Dunmore's advance was such a well-kept secret that General Skinner knew nothing of the immediate danger to the Albemarle.

All might have gone successfully for the British if it had not been for a brave sixteen-year-old girl who heard by chance of Lord Dunmore's plans. Betsy Dowdy lived with her father on the Currituck County banks just below the Virginia line. It was already dark on a bitterly cold night when she overheard a neighbor tell her father about the peril North Carolina faced. Worst of all, she learned that her beloved ponies were to be rounded up and taken away. Immediately she knew what she had to do. She had to get word to General Skinner. Leaving a note for her father, she went outside and called softly to her favorite pony, Black Bess, and leaped up on the sturdy little mare. The race was on. First scampering down the sandbanks, next swimming the frigid water of Currituck Sound to the mainland, the brave pair swept across the insecure terrain of the Dismal Swamp, then past Camden and Elizabeth City and Hertford. Finally at daybreak Betsy Dowdy and Black Bess reached General Skinner's headquarters.

Upon receiving the news, the general acted promptly, marched to meet the British, and defeated them at the Battle of Great Bridge. Northeastern North Carolina was saved, and so were the Banker ponies. After a much-needed rest Betsy and Black Bess returned to the Currituck banks and Betsy's proud father. Over the years, storytellers have never forgotten Betsy Dowdy and her lonely fifty-mile ride one icy night to save her people and her ponies.

Mary Slocum's Dream

One of the first battles of the American Revolution was fought at Moores Creek Bridge in southeastern North Carolina. A sizable band of loyalists had left Cross Creek (now Fayetteville) and were moving toward Brunswick to join the royal governor. In the foggy dawn of February 27, 1776, the loyalists were intercepted by a small army of American patriots and were defeated at Moores Creek Bridge. Among the victorious Americans was sixteen-year-old Lieutenant Ezekiel Slocumb.

On the Sunday night before the battle, his equally young wife Mary was sleeping restlessly, her thoughts on her husband who had left home only that morning. She tossed and turned, and then she had a dream. "I saw distinctly a body wrapped in my husband's guard-cloak, bloody, dead," she later said, "and others dead and wounded on the ground about him. . . . I uttered a cry and sprang to my feet on the floor." She placed her tiny baby in the care of a trustworthy servant, ran to the barn, saddled her mare, and in a moment "was tearing down the road at full speed." For sixty miles she sped south, never slackening the pace.

At daybreak Mary heard sounds of a battle. She hurried on, and on a bank near the road, "under a cluster of trees, were lying, perhaps, twenty men. They were the wounded. I knew the spot; the very trees; and the position of the men I knew, as if I had seen it a thousand times. I had seen it in my dreams all night! I saw it all at once; but in an instant, my whole soul was centered in one spot; for there, wrapped in his bloody guard-cloak, was my husband's body!" She jumped from the mare and tore aside the garment. It was not her husband but another man badly wounded. "I took his knife, cut away his trousers and stocking, and found the blood came from a hole shot through and through the fleshy part of his leg. I looked and could see nothing as if it would do for dressing wounds but some heart leaves. I gathered a handful and bound them tight to the holes, and the bleeding stopped." She then moved to the next form stretched out on the ground, and the next and the next. So intent was she in caring for the wounded that there was no time to inquire about her husband.

After many hours, she heard a familiar voice and looking up from her crouching position, she saw Ezekiel standing there, "as bloody as a butcher and as muddy as a ditcher" but not seriously injured. He had just returned to his unit from pursuing the enemy.

"Why, Mary," he cried out, "what are you doing here?" Though he was completely surprised, he was indeed happy to see her and proud of her work with his wounded comrades.

At nightfall, Mary decided to return home. Ezekiel and the commanding general attempted to dissuade her, promising to send her back the following morning with an escort. But she said no, she needed to be with her baby, and off she flew on her mare sixty miles through the dark night. "What a happy ride I had!" she confessed, "and with what joy did I embrace my child!"

A gourd dipper, said to be the one Mary Slocumb kept fastened to her saddle during the famous ride, is on exhibit at the Museum of History in Raleigh.

The Little Red Man

The best known Salem ghost is the Little Red Man, once a familiar figure in the Brothers House, if tradition may be believed. The queer part about this story is that its origin was neither in crime nor in mystery, and a proper ghost story should have either the one or the other as foundation. Here is what really happened, as noted in the official record of the death of Andreas Kremser, the entry standing as No. 45 in the Church Book of Salem Congregation:

The Single Brother, Andreas Kremser, departed early in the morning of March 26, in the Brothers House here, and was buried on the 27th in our God's Acre.

He was born March 7, 1753, in Gnadenhutten in Pennsylvania, and from his third year was brought up in the home and school for little boys, first in Bethlehem and then in Nazarath.

In October, 1766, he came to North Carolina. In Bethabara he worked as a shoe-maker; and on Feb. 6, 1772, he moved to Salem.

On the 25th of March, 1786, he attended the festival services of the congregation and of his choir but was uncommonly quiet all day. After the evening service several of the Brethren decided to work for a while on excavating the cellar for an addition to the Brothers House. They used the method which had been employed successfully in similar cases, that is they undercut a bank and then pulled down the overhang. Several Brethren doubted the advisability of doing that here, because of the more sandy character of the soil, but few agreed with them.

About half past eleven Brother Kremser was warned by a Brother who found him kneeling at this work, but he could not see the danger. About twelve o'clock, midnight, a Brother who was watching overhead saw that a great bank was breaking, and called to the men working below to jump back, which they did, and no one was much hurt except our Brother Kremser, who could not get away quickly because he was on his knees. He was covered by the falling earth and quite buried in it. He was dug out as quickly as possible, and was then still alive, and spoke, complaining of pain. It was evident that his left leg was broken. The doctor, Brother Lewis, opened a vein in his arm, but little blood flowed, and there were soon signs of his approaching departure, which followed about two o'clock, the blessing of the Church having been given to him amid many tears.

This fatal accident in the midnight hour seems to have made a deep impression on the men living in the Brothers House; and thereafter, when an unusual sound was heard at night, especially it it resembled the tap-tap-tapping of a shoemaker's hammer, someone would whisper: "There's Kremser!" It is said that he was small of stature, and that he was wearing a red cap when the bank caved in on him, and now and then somebody would hear light steps hurrying through the hall, and occasionally someone would catch a glimpse of a little man in a red cap slipping past a door.

In the course of years changes came, and the building was no longer used as a home for the unmarried men of the community, but was occupied by some of the older women. Little Betsy often went thither to visit her grandmother. Now little Betsy had just learned to talk when a serious illness left her entirely deaf. She was tenderly cared for, knew nothing of accidents, death, or ghosts, but one day she came to her grandmother in some excitement, pointing to the hall and saying in her childish speech: "Betsy saw little man out there, and he did this at her," beckoning with her finger, as one child calls another to play. Was it a child's imagination or the Little Red Man? Who knows? The latter was the accepted version.

Years passed, and stories told by elderly ladies living in the house were received with a half smile until one day one of the substantial citizens of Salem showed a visitor through the interesting subcellars of the former Brothers House. He told the tradition of the Little Red Man, and suddenly there he was! The two men suddenly resolved to catch him, but their outstretched arms met around empty air, while the Little Red Man grinned at them from the doorway. The substantial citizen told the incident to the man who told me, so what more definite proof could be desired? Incidentally I might remark that the aforesaid substantial citizen was not addicted to the use of spirituous refreshments, so that otherwise obvious explanation will not suffice.

The present generation of residents in the old Brothers House declares that the Little Red Man no longer appears; and it is claimed that the termination of his activity was caused by a visiting minister, who, hearing the story, declared that he could "lay the ghost," and pronounced an invocation to the Trinity, adding the command: "Little Red Man, go to rest!" Since this was the most long-lived ghost that Salem has owned it seems an open question whether one should be grateful to the clergyman who exorcised him, or to the electric lights which have driven the shadows from the subcellars of the one-time Brothers House. (Adelaide L. Fries)

Old Quawk

Every year on a Saturday in mid-March Morehead City celebrates Old Quawk Day. Among the several events is a Quawk Calling Contest, in which expert squawkers vie for prizes. Contestants try to imitate the voice of Old Quawk, a fisherman on the Outer Banks in colonial times.

Old Quawk was a mean, disagreeable fellow who had come from a foreign country. For the Bankers, his last name was rather impossible to pronounce, and the closest they could come to it was Old Quawk. Besides, his voice was loud and grating like the squawky screech of a night heron. The name seemed to fit him. Yet there was one thing no one could deny: Old Quawk was an excellent fisherman.

On a certain Sunday morning—it was March 16—he hove into port with the largest catch anyone at the harbor had ever seen. It took quite a few men to help him remove the fish from his vessel. He bragged in a gruff way about his luck. And then he began to set sail to return to the open sea. "This time I'll bring in even more," he growled.

The other fishermen tried to get him to change his mind. They reminded him it was Sunday, and it was a sin to fish on Sunday. They warned him that the weather signs were ominous and that he could expect a storm at sea.

"I care nothing about sin! I care nothing about storms! I care nothing that it is Sunday!" he yelled above the rising wind. "Wait here at the dock if you want to see the biggest catch in all the history of fishing on the Banks! For I am greater and more powerful than any God in heaven!" And with that, he sailed away from the safe harbor and into the rough ocean, followed by a shrieking night heron.

Old Quawk was never seen again, and March 16 was set aside to remind humbler folk of the dangers which beset defiant men and of the power of God and nature.

The Devil's Tramping Ground

In a wooded area in western Chatham County, ten miles east of Siler City, is a well-worn path that forms a ring forty feet in diameter. The path itself is a foot wide. The center of the circle and the ground outside the path are lush with grass and other plant life, but nothing grows in the foot-wide track. At sunset, when rocks or similar heavy objects are placed in the pathway, they are found the next morning to have been brushed aside. In fall and winter, when rabbit hunters roam the surrounding countryside, their dogs perform joyously until the chase nears the barren circle. Then the dogs tuck their tails between their legs and slink away. They will not go near the spot.

Soon after the first settlers came to Chatham County, they discovered the strange site, which soon became known as the Devil's Tramping Ground. This was before 1800.

Though no one ever saw him stalking there, it was believed to be the haunt of the Foul Fiend, who came at night to tramp around and around and around in a circle, his head lowered, his expression intense. It was during these hours that Satan planned his evil schemes to undo mankind. At first light of morning he was gone, winging his way like a bat across the world to carry out his nefarious purposes. Yet so scorching had been his footprints on the ground of his circular pathway that the soil became infertile, and the nocturnal retreat of the hellish Prince of Darkness was shunned and avoided.

Young Andrew Jackson's Skylarking

Yes, he became president of the United States. And yes, in his young manhood he studied law in Salisbury and then traveled on horseback from one courthouse to the next in western North Carolina practicing his newly learned profession. Andrew Jackson was always jolly, always playing practical jokes and participating in sporting activities, always having the time of his life. Aristocratic girls from the plantations frightened him unreasonably, but he managed to enjoy himself anyway.

One warm summer evening in Salisbury, a ball was being held at the Rowan Inn. Members of society from town and county were on hand. The hall was beautifully decorated. Chaperones sat along the wall and watched the swaying figures of dainty girls and handsome men sweep about the dance floor. Sumptuous refreshments were spread out on several tables.

Not dancing that evening but standing in a corner was a slender, rawboned fellow about twenty years old. It was Andrew Jackson, of course. As the couples glided past, many a girl smiled at him invitingly, but he made no motion to secure a partner. He kept one eye on the door, the other on the busy young ball manager.

As the hour neared midnight, two not so young women, gaudily dressed, their faces painted garishly, appeared and presented their admission cards. The doorkeeper knew who they were and, as politely as he could, prevented them from entering. The music stopped, the dancers froze, the chaperones glared at the intruders, and the ball manager rushed over to the women. He looked at the admission cards; they were genuine, no mistake about it. "There must be some error," he said to them. "Where did you get these cards?" The "ladies" smiled roguishly. "For sure," they replied, "Mister Andrew Jackson presented them to us." And with that they moved into the center of the ballroom floor.

Mothers and fathers gathered up their dainty daughters, escorts picked up wraps, and all made a hasty exit from the Rowan Inn. No one moved threateningly toward the perpetrator of the joke, for his reputation as a fighter was only too well known. In a few moments the room was empty except for the fellow in the corner and the two inelegant women. Prancing delightedly toward them, the young lawyer made a low bow and led his invitees to their carriage in the now empty street.

Jackson's dislike of pretense and "high society" remained with him right through his eight years in the White House, as did his love of masculine frivolity.

As a young attorney, he relished the legal bouts in the little county seats of Salisbury, Charlotte, Lincolnton, and Morganton. In between sessions of court, he was present whenever and wherever there was any horse racing or cockfighting. As he rode along from one court session to the next, he held fast to a little blue rooster, as frisky and fighting a creature as its owner. In and around Morganton one of his sporting companions was dignified Colonel Waightstill Avery. But that was before Jackson challenged Avery to a duel. The calm and assured colonel allowed Jackson to fire first. The shot was wide. Then Avery walked over to the hotheaded fellow and gave him a fatherly lecture on his overhasty defiance.

After a while, Jackson decided to move to the new state of Tennessee, and struck out on the Yellow Mountain Road in today's Avery County to get there. On blustery nights, some people say, the ghost of Andrew Jackson can be seen charging up and down the Yellow Mountain Road, waving his sword and holding fast to a little blue rooster.

President Washington and Betsy Brandon

During President George Washington's first term he decided to go on a journey throughout the South to meet the citizens and learn something of their problems and needs. In late spring he set out and was greeted everywhere with fanfare and ceremony. On May 30, 1791, he was on his way from Charlotte to Salisbury, where a great banquet was to be held in his honor. Everyone of importance in Rowan County was to be present, and among those invited were Squire and Mrs. Richard Brandon. They arose at sunrise, put on their best clothes, and were soon off to the county seat six miles away.

Left at home were fourteen-year-old Betsy Brandon and Charity, the cook. Betsy was of course disappointed that she would not be able to see the famous man. As she thought of the fine food to be spread out on the banquet tables in Salisbury, she looked dejectedly at her simple repast of hoecake and buttermilk. "Oh, Charity," she said, "what wouldn't I give to dine with President Washington!" She felt alone and neglected.

At that moment she heard a knock on the door. Upon opening it, she was greeted by an elderly man. "My coach broke down," he explained, "and while the wheel is being repaired, I would like to rest in your pleasant home." The hospitable Betsy invited him in. "Where are your parents?" he asked.

"They have gone off to Salisbury to see the president, but I was not allowed to go. More than anything in the world I would like to dine with the president."

"Well," said the elderly man, "we shall see about that. But just now, I am rather hungry myself. What are you having for breakfast?"

Though Betsy was ashamed to tell him, she knew she must be honest. "Only hoecake and buttermilk," she replied.

"May I dine with you? I like hoecake and buttermilk."

And so it was that Betsy Brandon and the elegant old gentleman sat down to breakfast. Charity brought in the simple fare.

"Are you going to Salisbury to see the president?" asked Betsy.

"Oh, I have seen him many times. And you know, this is the very best hoecake and buttermilk I have ever had."

A messenger arrived to say that the coach wheel had been repaired. The elderly man got up from the table, thanked the girl again, then

paused at the doorway. "Don't be sad," he said, "for I am George Washington, and you have dined with the president before anyone else in all of Rowan County."

Roan Mountain and Its Music

All sorts of strange things are told about Roan Mountain, a mile-high peak in Mitchell County lying astride the dividing line between Tennessee and North Carolina.

For one thing, it is a mountain "bald," and no trees grow on the top of it. The story is told that the Catawba Indians once challenged all their enemies to come there and fight. Though the Catawbas won in three gory battles, so much blood was shed that the trees withered away and never grew back, and the rhododendron which gradually took hold on the heights had blossoms mostly crimson in hue.

Sometimes the fierce wind pounds the mountain so hard that it blows holes in the northwest side. Or so it is said. On calmer days, after a thunderstorm, a rainbow appears—not a semicircular one, but a completely round one.

And what about the ghostly music that early travelers heard? To some it seemed like the humming of a thousand bees. Others thought it sounded rather like the constant low snapping of one glass jar upon another and was merely an electrical phenomenon resulting from two powerful winds meeting head-on in a narrow gap on the mountain.

Yet no scientific explanation has ever convinced the local folk that it is not the heavenly melody of angels practicing for Judgment Day.

At Chimney Rock

Long, long ago the deep gorge below Chimney Rock was the home of the Little People. They hated the Cherokee Indians and would not let them travel through the gorge on their way to buy tobacco down in the low country. To make safe the passage through the mountains, a Cherokee magician changed himself into a whirlwind, then blew himself in a fury through the gorge, scattering huge rocks in every direction. So frightened were the Little People that they left their home and were not seen again for centuries. In time, the Indians also disappeared from the country, and the white settlers came into the gap between the mountains.

On July 31, 1806, two children were playing in a field below Chimney Rock. Elizabeth Reaves, age eight, looked up and saw a man on the Rock picking up sticks. She told her brother Morgan, age eleven; and when Morgan turned his eyes upward, he saw "a thousand or ten thousand things flying in the air." Had the Little People come back? Elizabeth and Morgan called their mother from her cabin, and she too witnessed a crowd of humanlike figures swarming over and around the Rock. They were of various sizes, some tall men, others small infants, but all clothed in "brilliant white raiment." A few rose up from the Rock, then dropped down upon it. This went on for an hour. A neighbor was sent for and he, too, observed the figures. Suddenly they

were gone and a great rainbow spread across the heavens.

At sunset one evening five years later, an old man and his wife living in the gap were looking at the sky when all at once they saw two armies of horsemen in the air above Chimney Rock. The armies met head-on, and the two old people heard the clashing of swords, the cries of the wounded. After ten minutes the defeated army left the scene, and shouts of the victors resounded throughout the valley. Neighbors saw and heard them too. Then all was quiet again. Were these the Little People once more, or other strange inhabitants of Chimney Rock?

The Honeymoon

In the first years of the nineteenth century, there lived in the hill country of North Carolina a noble but poor young farmer and carpenter named George Bolton. After he and beautiful Mary Lawton fell in love, he chose a pleasant site on a hillside where he began building a house for his bride-to-be. The spot was protected by handsome shade trees, and a spring of pure cool water was nearby. A large flat rock, though pocketed with small holes, served as floor and hearth for the modest dwelling.

The cottage was completed in mid-December. "I shall light no fire on my hearth," said George to himself, "till I bring Mary here to be warmed by its heat."

After the marriage one cold evening during the Christmas holidays, the young couple went directly to their new home, started a scorching fire on the stone hearth, and retired. In the middle of the night they were awakened by strange noises. The fire had died down, and George leaped from the bed to put more wood on it.

He stepped upon something alive, something writhing and coiling about his feet. Looking down, he discovered himself surrounded by fifty or more wriggling rattlesnakes. He felt the sharp bites as he dropped to the floor among them, shouting to Mary in the last moment of his life, "Cover yourself with the blanket! Stay where you are! Don't move!"

And then there was no sound—no sound but the odious clatter of the serpents. The horror-stricken Mary pulled the blankets about her. The snakes crept upon the bed and glided back and forth over her as the slow night wore on.

When neighbors came and forced open the door, the first thing they saw was George's swollen body, lying amid the snakes now sluggish in the morning chill. They were promptly killed. Mary was rescued, but overnight her dark hair had turned white, and her smooth, rosy complexion had become wrinkled and ashen.

Unknown to George Bolton, beneath the stone hearth the hibernating snakes had been warmed into life by the blazing fire and had squirmed through the holes into the heated room.

The Portrait of Theodosia Burr

On December 31, 1812, the beautiful and vivacious Theodosia Burr, wife of wealthy Governor Joseph Alston of South Carolina, left her husband's plantation and sailed north on the *Patriot* to visit her beloved father, the famous Aaron Burr, in New York City. In early January the vessel was accosted off Cape Hatteras by ships of Great Britain, then at war with the United States, but was permitted to proceed on its journey. The *Patriot* was never seen again nor, with any certainty, was Theodosia.

An angry storm that very night swept the coast of North Carolina. Some say that during the gale pirates boarded the *Patriot*, removed all valuables, forced passengers and crew to walk the plank, then sank the ship. But legend persists that Theodosia survived, that she was cast ashore in a small boat onto the Outer Banks, bereft of all possessions except a portrait of herself, and that, with her sanity completely gone, she was thereafter cared for by a Banker fisherman and his wife.

The years went by. In 1869 the strange woman became ill, and a doctor from Elizabeth City was called in to attend her. He did what he could, but it was clear that she had not long to live. As he was leaving the sick room, the poor fisherman's wife told the doctor that, as she had no money, he would have to choose something from the house for his pay. When he replied that he would like to have the handsome portrait hanging on the wall, the afflicted old woman sprang from the bed. "It is mine! You shall not have it! I am on my way to visit my father in New York, and I am taking him this picture of his darling

Theodosia!" With that, she grabbed the canvas, rushed through the door, ran down to the surf, and walked into the ocean. The next day, the portrait washed up on the beach.

It is fact, not legend, that the doctor took the picture from Nags Head to his home in Elizabeth City, that a descendant sold it to an art dealer who in turn sold it to a member of the Burr family, and that it exists today.

A Speech for Buncombe

From 1817 to 1823, western North Carolina, including the proud county of Buncombe, sent Felix Walker to the House of Representatives in Washington. He was a glib and garrulous talker, and doubtless it was his very trivial and high-sounding speeches that found favor with the word-loving mountain voters of the day.

On February 25, 1820, during the congressional debate on the Missouri Compromise, Walker signaled that he wished to make a speech. But so protracted had been the debate and so weary were the members of the House that a colleague told Walker that no one wished to hear him at that time. The persistent fellow said that he would take only a few moments, for he wished merely a chance to get his speech reported in the newspapers and in that way provide his constituents with solid evidence that he was doing a good job in Washington. "I shall not be speaking to the House," he confessed, "but to Buncombe."

But in the chambers of the House, "the question was called for so clamorously and so perseveringly that Mr. W. could proceed no farther than to move that the Committee rise," which it refused to do. When later the representative delivered his oration and had it printed in the newspaper, it was agreed that truly it was a speech for Buncombe, meaning that it was frivolous, repetitious, and unnecessary.

Felix Walker was not downcast. He had done the thing he needed to do, and that was that. Came the comment: "Walker's speech was *buncombe*—no doubt about it."

The word caught on. Eventually it was spelled *bunkum*, meaning any nonsensical language, then shortened to *bunk*. In such a way did a beautiful mountain county in North Carolina add a new and useful word to the English dictionary.

❦

Peter Stewart Ney, Schoolmaster

In the early 1820s a strange red-haired man came to North Carolina. He was of powerful physique, had sword scars on his face, played the flute, wrote poetry, and was accomplished in Latin and French. In Davie, Rowan, and adjoining counties, he soon took up residence in the homes of well-to-do cotton planters, where he would set up a schoolroom to teach the children of the neighborhood. He usually kept to himself, and only when he was drinking would he speak of his past. At night he wrote in a journal and read histories of France, in the margins of which he would make corrections. He read the local newspapers avidly, particularly the dispatches from Europe. When told of the death of Napoleon Bonaparte, he fell to the floor in a fainting spell, and a few hours later attempted suicide. In Mocksville he challenged a French fencing instructor many years his junior and easily defeated the expert.

Sometimes he would tell his students that he was not the simple Scottish schoolmaster they believed him to be, but Marshal Michel Ney, Napoleon's friend and second in command, whose supposed execution in Paris in 1815 had been faked. With the help of friends, he said, he had escaped and had come to live in America until the day when Emperor Napoleon regained his throne. Napoleon's death ended all plans to return to Europe.

In truth, the teacher looked much like the picture of Michel Ney, marshal of France. The red hair and the scars seemed to be identical. Penmanship of the two was apparently the same. Peter Stewart Ney scoffed at evidence that the execution of Marshal Ney was not a deception. On his deathbed in 1846 at the age of seventy-seven, he was asked for this last time if he was Napoleon's marshal. "Yes," he replied. "I will not die with a lie on my lips! I am Marshal Ney of France!"

But was he? He was buried in the cemetery of the Third Creek Presbyterian Church in Rowan County. His design for the Davidson College official seal is still in use.

How Nags Head Got Its Name

In early days on the Outer Banks, settlers were isolated and provisions hard to come by. During seasons when the sea was unresponsive and when the catch was low, hungry fishermen looked longingly at the richly laden ships sweeping up and down the coast between

Charleston and the northern ports. At these times, a few desperate men turned land pirates. On stormy nights they tied a lantern to the neck of a nag—one of the many Banker ponies roaming the dunes and marshes—and led him along the beach. Ships at sea saw the light and, thinking it a signal from some vessel rocking back and forth in a snug and safe harbor, steered toward the beam hoping to find refuge from the destructive waves.

Too late they found themselves in the midst of swirling, ferocious breakers. The ships crashed upon the beach, the crews were drowned, the cargoes scattered along the sands. The land pirates recovered from the wreck whatever they could use at home or whatever they could sell to unsuspecting buyers. Mariners soon avoided that section of the coastline which came to be called Nags Head.

Not so, says another legend. The beach was called Nags Head because the outline of the dunes thereabouts, when observed at a certain angle from a fisherman's boat, resembles the head of a horse.

No, no, says the researcher. The place was given its name by English settlers from the old country who were quite familiar with the designation Nags Head. Many North Carolina place names came from Old England. In London, for instance, just behind the Royal Opera House, Covent Garden, is a popular pub called The Nags Head, and it has been right there in that spot, whereof the memory of man runneth not to the contrary. Nags Head Creek, a tiny stream between Exeter and Cullompton, is in Devon, and everybody knows that many North Carolina settlers came from Devon. Then, too, there is a promontory known to sailors as Nags Head, which juts out from the westernmost of the Isles of Scilly in Cornwall. A large rock formation there resembles a horse's head. A lot of early North Carolinians also came from Cornwall.

Maybe so, maybe so, replies the folklorist, who goes on believing that wicked land pirates once tied a lantern to a nag's head and lured ships to their destruction on stormy nights.

Peter Dromgoole

On the eastern edge of Chapel Hill, near where the highway to Raleigh plunges down an incline into the Triassic basin, stands medieval-like Gimghoul Castle, and just in front of the doorway to the castle is a large rounded rock circled today by boxwoods. On the surface of the rock are dark rusty stains.

It seems that a student named Peter Dromgoole, from Lawrenceville, Virginia, entered the University of North Carolina in 1830. He was a high-strung fellow, fond of gambling and drinking and horse racing. He was aristocratic, proud, and defiant. By the end of his second year he was deeply in love with a girl in the village named Miss Fannie. The only trouble was that Miss Fannie had another devoted suitor. During the commencement ball on a soft moonlit night in the early summer of 1832, Peter Dromgoole and his rival spoke some violent words to each other, and it was agreed that the two would meet half a mile away on Piney Prospect (where Gimghoul Castle now stands) and let their pistols decide which one of them would claim Miss Fannie.

Though duels were of course outlawed, they walked briskly at midnight to the appointed spot, accompanied by their seconds. Miss Fannie had somehow learned what was to happen, and she appeared on the scene just as the signal was given and the shots rang out in the air. Peter Dromgoole fell across a large rounded rock, his blood pouring out and staining the surface of the stone. Miss Fannie crumpled in a faint to the ground. As she was being carried away, the frightened students dug a hasty grave for Peter Dromgoole near the rock, and the next day they hurriedly left the university village for their distant homes.

As summer wore on, Miss Fannie became weaker and weaker. Occasionally she visited the scene of the tragedy, but finally her health kept her confined to her room. One evening she was heard to whisper, "I'm going to him—he's sad—alone, alone," and then she died, believing that she would meet her beloved Peter Dromgoole.

At midnight in early summer when the moon is full, Miss Fannie and Peter Dromgoole walk arm and arm together under the tall pine trees at Gimghoul Castle. Many students claim to have seen them there.

Long Time between Drinks

The Nancy Jones House is a white two-story clapboarded structure built in 1805 three miles beyond Cary on the old road between Raleigh and Morrisville. It has a steeply pitched gable roof, exterior end chimneys, and double-gallery entrance portico with pediment. A windmill stands behind the house.

The long-undiscovered diary of Mrs. Ann (called Nancy) Jones describes a widely quoted incident. On a hot summer day in 1838, Governor Edward B. Dudley of North Carolina and Governor Pierce M. Butler of South Carolina arrived at the same time, were ushered into the parlor and served tall cool mint juleps. Lany, the maid, and the houseboy ran to mix more juleps but not quickly enough for the thirsty governors.

Lany reentered the room as the governor of North Carolina was saying to the governor of South Carolina: "It's a damn long time between drinks."

"Damn long!" his companion replied.

When Mrs. Jones heard of the remark from the scandalized maid, she was shocked and embarrassed at the implied reflection on her hospitality.

Another version has been handed down in the family of John Motley Morehead, minister to Sweden (1930-1933), whose grandfather was governor of North Carolina (1841-1845). After futile correspondence between Governor Morehead, a Whig, and Governor James Henry Hammond of South Carolina, a Democrat, concerning the extradition of a political offender, the two officials met with their staffs and legal advisers for a conference on the state line, not far from Charlotte. During the discussion Governor Hammond became excited and finally announced that further refusal would result in his sending a military force into North Carolina to seize the fugitive.

"Now, sir," he shouted, crashing his fist upon the table, "what is your answer?"

"My reply, sir," answered Governor Morehead with great deliberation, "is this: It's a damn long time between drinks."

This unexpected answer had the effect of so relieving the tension that the two governors were able to talk dispassionately and eventually to reach a settlement satisfactory to both states. (Blackwell P. Robinson)

Specter at the Gold Mine

During the Carolina gold rush of the 1830s and 1840s, a miserly old codger called Skinflint McIntosh owned a rich vein in southern Cabarrus County. So tightfisted was he that he wouldn't pay adequate wages to the miners to dig for the gold, nor would he provide sufficient safety measures to prevent accidents in his mine. The vein of gold was 450 feet down a narrow shaft.

One of the best workers in the district was Joe McGee, whom Skinflint kept trying to hire. "If I got killed down there," said Joe, "would you pay my wife Jennie $1,000?" "Joe," Skinflint shouted, "I'd pay her $2,000." And so it was that Joe gave up his other job and went to work for Skinflint.

One cold, drizzly night, when Joe didn't come home at the usual hour, Jennie became worried. Finally she persuaded Joe's friend Shaun to gather up a few men and look for Joe in the mine. They searched the deep hole but found nothing. After several weeks Jennie asked Skinflint for her money. "Oh, no," said Skinflint, "Joe's just gone off somewhere." And he didn't pay her.

Soon after, on another bitter night, a loud knock came on Shaun's door. Opening it, he was startled by a ghastly white specter who spoke with the voice of his friend Joe and told Shaun to go to the mine that very night; it told him to dig at a certain spot where the green timbers had given away and caused a cave-in. It asked if Skinflint had paid Jennie, and when Shaun said no, the specter wailed, "I'll haunt that mine of his forever."

McGee's body was found exactly where the specter said. Skinflint paid up, but only when threatened by Joe's old friends. Word spread about the haunted mine, and no one would work for McIntosh. All of this happened 150 years ago but the gold is still in the mine—as is the specter of Joe McGee.

Jesse Holmes the Foolkiller

Every town and county and state and nation needs a Foolkiller— that is, a fellow who becomes so exasperated with the stupidity of idiots and rascals that he goes about knocking them on the head with his always-at-hand "death-dealing club." In the middle of the nineteenth century, one of the citizens of the village of Milton in Caswell County was such a fellow. His name was Jesse Holmes. He was an angry little man who turned on fools wherever he found them, and "slathered" them but good. Furthermore, he wrote letters to the local newspaper telling of his exploits. (That he never really existed but sprang from the fertile mind of Charles Napoleon Bonaparte Evans, editor of the *Milton Chronicle*, is neither here nor there.)

With his mighty jo-darter, the Foolkiller sought out numskulls, spreading them out "as flat as a pancake." He wrote to the *Chronicle* that, among others, he slew "frisky old widowers," a young man planning to marry a girl not for love but for money, "worthless" members of the state legislature, a "bandy-shanked lark" sleeping in church with his "mouth open and full of flies," some nincompoops standing around waiting for a man to ascend in a balloon with a six-horse wagon and team, and an "old farmer" who told "a young man how to take warts off his hands, the advice being to cut one more notch on the north side of a persimmon tree than he had warts."

This brave little folk figure soon passed from the columns of the *Chronicle* into the wide realm of American folklore. He was known and loved everywhere but his origin was forgotten. For example, O. Henry in his short story "The Fool-Killer" seems not to have been aware that Jesse Holmes was, like himself, a native North Carolinian.

Siren of the French Broad River

Among the rocks [near Asheville] lives the Lorelei of the French Broad River. This stream—the Tselica of the Indians—contains in its upper reaches many pools where the rapid water whirls and deepens, where the traveller likes to pause in the heat of afternoon and drink and bathe. Here, from the time when the Cherokee occupied the country, has lived the siren, and if one who is weary and downcast sits beside the stream or utters a wish to rest in it, he becomes conscious of a soft and exquisite music blending with the splash of the wave.

Looking down in surprise he sees—at first faintly, then with distinctness—the form of a beautiful woman, with hair streaming like moss and dark eyes looking into his, luring him with a power he cannot resist. His breath grows short, his gaze is fixed, mechanically he rises, steps to the brink, and lurches forward into the river. The arms that catch him are slimy and cold as serpents; the face that stares into his is a grinning skull. A loud, chattering laugh rings through the wilderness, and all is still again. (Charles M. Skinner)

Brown Mountain Lights

As mountains go, low-lying Brown Mountain in Burke County is not impressive. Yet it is one of the most famous mountains in North Carolina. On certain evenings soon after dark, when observed from the eminence of Linville or Wiseman's Gap, small but brilliant lights can be seen on it, bobbing up and down for a minute or so, then disappearing, then reappearing in another place until finally they are gone. They were first seen about 1850 long before the day of trains and electricity and automobiles.

One legend tells of a girl who lived on the mountain with her father. Every night her sweetheart came from the village to see her, tramping through a forest of snakes and vicious animals. On the evening when he was to take her away to be married, she lighted a pine torch and went out to welcome him. He never came. But from then on, at sunset, she raised her flaming torch and darted from here to there on the mountain, hoping to come upon him. After her death the light of her torch still could be seen on stormy nights.

Another legend concerns a wicked man named Jim, whose sweet-tempered young wife Belinda was to have a child. Jim was courting Susie and began to speak harsh words and be cruel to Belinda. One

day neighbors noticed that they had not seen Belinda for some while. Jim said she had gone to visit her kinfolk, but the neighbors were suspicious when they discovered bloodstains on the floor of the mountain cabin. Their suspicions were further heightened when an indigent stranger drove away with Jim's horse and wagon. They believed the stranger had helped Jim kill and bury Belinda, and Jim was paying him off in this way. Soon afterward the lights appeared, bobbing up and down, seemingly to guide searchers looking for Belinda. Finally, under a pile of stones in a deep ravine they found the skulls of a woman and a baby. Jim left the county and was never heard of again, but the lights stayed on, reminding evildoers that their crimes will be revealed.

Apart from the legends, scientists have provided many explanations for the mysterious Brown Mountain Lights, none of them satisfactory.

The Witch Bride

Many years ago in Northampton County, a man married a young woman who was a witch. The young husband made this startling discovery soon after the wedding. A few nights after the marriage vows had been spoken, the man awoke and asked, "Honey, are you asleep?" Receiving no reply, he realized his wife was not at his side, whereupon he got out of bed and to his horror saw his bride's skin hanging across a chair.

Much grieved to learn he had indeed married a witch, the hapless fellow knew he must catch his witch wife, even though he still loved her. Several nights later, pretending sleep, he saw her take off her skin and heard her say, "Devil be with me and out I go!" Immediately she vanished through the keyhole of the door.

The husband seized this opportunity to rub the witch's skin with red pepper; then he went back to bed. Just before daybreak he heard someone say, "Devil be with me and in I go!" With that the woman slipped back into her skin and went to bed, but she began to roll and tumble, unable to go to sleep. Day dawned and then the witch could not get out of her skin to remove the pepper. She grew gravely ill, went out of her mind, and died later that day.

["The Witch Bride" is from F. Roy Johnson, who adds this note: "In a similar Hertford County tale a witch was likewise trapped. She couldn't stay in her burning skin; and her husband seized her by the hair, threw her into the heater and burned her up. He was not unhappy. He got another wife who was not a witch."—The editor.]

Tar Heels

In the early days North Carolina was noted for the tar and turpentine produced in the broad pine barrens of the coastal plain, and its inhabitants were nicknamed Tar Burners and Tar Boilers. Then, during the Civil War, soldiers from North Carolina got to be known as Tar Heels.

At first the term was insulting. Tradition has it that soldiers from other states used the words *Tar Heels* to make fun of the poor, ignorant, often barefoot North Carolina troops, sometimes with tar on their heels from working in the pine forests. Then the day came when some Virginians and South Carolinians had been driven from the field in a fierce battle, while the North Carolinians held fast.

When the groups met again, the deserters, wishing to make light of their own cowardly actions, called out, "Any more tar down in the Old North State, boys?"

The answer came back, "No, not a bit. Old Jeff Davis has bought it all up."

Said a South Carolinian, "Is that so? What's he going to do with it?"

A proud Tar Heel replied, "He's going to put it on you'ns heels to make you stick better in the next fight."

When General Robert E. Lee heard about this, he said, "God bless the Tar Heel boys!"

From then on, Tar Heel was not an insulting term, but one of which North Carolinians boasted. Especially was this so after Governor Zebulon B. Vance, on a visit to his beloved soldiers in camp near the battlefields of northern Virginia, began his speech in this way: "I do not know how to address you boys. I can't say fellow citizens because none of us are citizens of this state of Virginia. I cannot say fellow soldiers because I am not one of you. Therefore, I have concluded to address you as fellow Tar Heels." The wild shouts of approval almost deafened Vance.

Thereafter someone made up a little song which went like this:

> I'm a raw recruit in a brand new suit,
> Nine hundred dollars bounty;
> And I've come to here from a Tar Heel town
> To fight for North Caroliny.

The Evil Hunter of Purgatory Mountain

In 1971 the site chosen for the new North Carolina Zoo was 900-foot-high Purgatory Mountain, southeast of Asheboro in Randolph County. It is a rugged tract of dense thickets, tall trees, and large sharp rocks jutting from the unproductive soil. How Purgatory Mountain got its name goes back, some say, to the last year of the Civil War.

That part of Randolph County was settled by peace-loving Quakers who, despising slavery, wanted no part in the Confederate army. In 1864 so hard up was the South for soldiers that a rapacious recruiter called the Hunter was sent into the area to enlist any healthy males he could put his hands on. He rounded up twenty-two Quaker boys fourteen years old or younger, tied them together, and set out for Wilmington to turn them in. In the boys' minds there was only one thought: to escape. In the confusion in Wilmington, where it was evident that the downfall of the Confederacy was a matter of mere months, the boys managed to slip away, keep out of sight, and arrive back in Randolph County. The evil Hunter was still there. Instead of returning to their parents' modest homes, where they knew they would be found by the Hunter, they hid out on Purgatory Mountain underneath the rocks and in the dense thickets.

Young though they were and schooled by their religious faith against killing, they had determined that the Hunter must be done away with. From their hideaways they observed his habits and noticed that always at daybreak he checked his fish traps on Richland Creek. Three of the older boys were chosen to kill him. One morning two shots rang out, and the man fell dead beside his fish traps.

The twenty-two boys were sworn to secrecy, and not a one of them ever repeated the names of the three lads who went out that morning, or the names of the two who fired the guns. But as they grew to manhood, they avoided hunting on Purgatory Mountain, where it was well known that the ghost of the Hunter, still in purgatory, was in search of his murderers—as he is today.

⚜︎

Traveling Church at Swan Quarter

Some people believe in miracles; some don't. I do, and so do the good folk down east at Swan Quarter, a low-lying village only a few feet above the waters of Pamlico Sound.

In the 1870s the Methodists of Swan Quarter decided to build a church. They chose a vacant lot that was conveniently situated and was the highest ground in the village. The building committee went to the owner of the lot and offered to purchase it. No, said the owner, he had other plans for the lot and wouldn't sell it at any price. The disappointed committee looked about for another site, found a less suitable one near the waterfront, and began to build their church.

In September, 1876, the church had been nearly completed when a violent hurricane swept in from the sound. On the second day of the storm, with the streets flooded to a depth of five feet, the still unfinished foundations of the church gave way. As the startled Methodists looked from their windows, they saw the church building floating like a ship. It lurched from its lot and sailed into the street, took its course as if a pilot were aboard, went on past the houses and stores, turned to the right at an intersection, moved into the vacant lot the committee had chosen in the first place, twisted around to face the street, and settled down.

It was all too much for the owner of the lot. He rowed his boat down the flooded street looking for the chairman of the building committee. He finally found him and told him to come to the courthouse the next morning. In no uncertain words, he promised then and there to sign a deed donating the lot to the Methodists. And the next morning it was done.

Today at Providence Church, appropriately named, is a sign which proclaims to one and all that it is "The Church moved by the hand of God."

Sop, Doll, Sop

Once upon a time, up in the North Carolina mountains, Jack was down on his luck, and he asked a miller for work. "Maybe you don't want this job," said the man, "because all my millers seem to die when they work here." Jack said, "I'd just as soon be dead as hungry and out of a job." The miller said all right, but that Jack would have to sleep and cook at the mill. That was fine with Jack.

That night he made a fire, baked some bread, fried some meat, and put his tin plate on the floor beside him to start eating. All of a sudden the room got dark as pitch, and Jack went over to build up the fire. He sat down again and looked around. The room was filled with twelve black cats. The biggest one put out its doll (paw), and said, "Sop, doll, sop," then started sopping up the bread and meat in Jack's plate.

"You do that again, and I'll cut your doll off," said Jack. The big cat did it again, and so Jack grabbed his knife and cut its right doll off. With that, all twelve black animals turned and scatted out of the mill in a hurry. The fire blazed up, and Jack saw that the cutoff paw had turned into a woman's hand with a ring on it.

The next morning the miller was late coming by because his wife was sick and he had been to eleven neighbors' houses to get women to come and nurse her. "Did you sleep well and get enough to eat last night?" said the miller. "Yes," said Jack, "except for one thing." And he told the miller what had happened and showed him the woman's hand. "Why, that's my wife's hand, and that ring is one I gave her yesterday."

With Jack tagging along, he went up to the house, glared at the eleven women, and told his wife to show him her hand. She pulled her left hand from the covers. "No, it's your right hand I want to see." She said she didn't have one.

"Why did you go down there last night?" he shouted at her. She said, "I didn't want you to have a miller. I wanted you to keep the mill yourself. And I got my friends and witched them into cats, and went down there to put poison in his sop." The miller turned to Jack. "I've been thinking my old woman was in with a gang of witches, but I didn't know she was the leader of them."

Jack and the miller shut all the doors and windows in the house, went out the front door and locked it, and set the house on fire, leaving the women inside.

"Them twelve witches," says the story, "started crackin' and poppin', and ever' one of 'em was burnt plumb up." From then on, Jack and the miller didn't have any more trouble down at the mill.

Maco Light

On a night in 1867, at the small Brunswick County station of Maco fifteen miles west of Wilmington, a slow freight train was puffing down the track. In the caboose was Joe Baldwin, the flagman. A jerking noise startled him, and he was aware that his caboose had become uncoupled from the rest of the train, which went heedlessly on its way. As the caboose slackened speed, Joe looked up and saw the beaming light of a fast passenger train bearing down upon him. Grab-

bing his lantern, he waved it frantically to warn the oncoming engineer of the imminent danger. It was too late. At a trestle over the swamp, the passenger train plowed into the caboose. Joe was decapitated: his head flew into the swamp on one side of the track, his lantern on the other. It was days before the destruction caused by the wreck was cleared away. And when Joe's head could not be found, his body was buried without it.

Thereafter on misty nights, Joe's headless ghost appeared at Maco, a lantern in its hand. Anyone standing at the trestle first saw an indistinct flicker moving up and down, back and forth. Then the beam swiftly moved forward, growing brighter and brighter as it neared the trestle. About fifty feet away it burst into a brilliant, burning radiance. After that, it dimmed, backed away down the track, and disappeared.

It was Joe and his lantern, of course. But what was he doing? Was he looking for his head? Or was he trying to signal an approaching train?

In 1889 President Grover Cleveland, on a political campaign, saw the mysterious light, as have hundreds of people throughout the years. But in 1977 when the railroad tracks were removed and the swamp reclaimed his haunting grounds, Joe seems to have lost interest in Maco. At least, he has not been seen there lately.

❧⁓⁓❧

Mystery Ship of Diamond Shoals

On the cold morning of January 31, 1921, a lookout at the Cape Hatteras Coast Guard Station reported that a five-masted schooner was stranded offshore on Diamond Shoals "with all sails set." Two boats went to her rescue, but the breakers were so turbulent that they could get only close enough to make out her name: *Carroll A. Deering*. There was no sign of a crew, and her lifeboats were missing. When she was finally boarded four days later, charts were found in disarray in the skipper's bathroom, and food, prepared but never eaten, was set out in the galley. The only thing alive was an unhappy, lonesome meowing yellow cat. Three weeks later the *Deering* was dynamited as a danger to shipping. What had happened?

Only a few facts have come to light. The *Deering* sailed from Boston in September, 1920, for Buenos Aires. Off Delaware the captain became sick and was replaced. Months later she began her homeward voyage from Buenos Aires, with Norfolk her destined port. In the West Indies the new captain told a friend he had no confidence in his crew. Later, the schooner lost her anchors in a storm somewhere off the mouth of the Cape Fear River. She was in trouble.

Was there a mutiny? Did the crew murder their unpopular captain and leave the ship in their lifeboats? Perhaps that is what happened. Or was the *Deering* captured by Russian pirates? For a while, rumor said that such was the case. A more likely story is that the disabled vessel, upon being stranded on Diamond Shoals, was abandoned by the captain and her eleven crewmen, and that subsequently the lifeboats were wrecked with all lives lost. Maybe so, but why were they in such a hurry that they left freshly cooked food untouched on their plates in the galley?

Bladenboro's Vampire Beast

Bladenboro, on the rich coastal plain of southeastern North Carolina, is normally a quiet farming and textile center. Nothing before or since has ever happened there like that week-long panic when a vampire beast terrified the place.

On December 29, 1953, a large black catlike animal with a round

face was sighted near the town as it dragged a dog into the under-
brush. Though the dog was drained of blood, almost none of its flesh
had been eaten. In the next few days three more dogs suffered the
same fate. Roy Fores, chief of police in Bladenboro, organized a
search party but came upon nothing in the swamp. After two more
blood-sucked dogs were found, the party made another vain search.
Their only discovery was "extremely large" tracks indicating claws an
inch long.

At nightfall, Bladenboro citizens began locking their doors and
staying inside their houses. What was "this thing"? A black panther?
A large bobcat? A rabid dog or wolf? And why only blood? Audacious
men went out with their hunting dogs, one of which was attacked only
a hundred feet away from the pack and dragged yelping into the
swamp.

On the next night, Lloyd Clemmons, who lived not far away, was at
home eating supper when he heard his dogs growling. Looking out of
the window, he saw "this thing" slinking away in the darkness. It was,
said Clemmons, three feet long, twenty inches high, with a long tail
and a cat's face. That same night a woman down the road was attacked by "this thing" as she stepped from her door.

Following reports in the newspapers about the vampire beast,
professional hunters arrived by the hundreds. Only a rabbit was
found, its head bitten off, its blood sucked. Hunters and curious spec-
tators now numbered about a thousand, and Chief Fores called off the
search, fearing the sharpshooters would start killing each other and
the bystanders. There were a few more incidents, and then the scare
died away. The mystery of the vampire beast has never been solved,
but memories of the week-long horror live on in Bladenboro.

Paul Green Hears about the Harnett Hag

The windshield wipers kept wunk-wunking, sweeping away the rain as we drove along. Some two or three miles beyond Buies Creek my friend Malcolm gestured off to the left.

"There's a story connected with that place out there all right," he said.

"What place?" I said, as I looked out across the rain-streaked field.

"See that thicket by the hedge row over there? A house used to stand there, long, long ago. Aunt Sarah McLean, an old black woman, told me about it. A man by the name of Baldy Ryalls lived there. One evening he went down below the hill to feed his hogs,and while they were eating the corn and the mash out of the trough, up come a snow-white deer from the woods close by and begun to eat the mash and stuff away from the hogs. Baldy run back to the house and got his old gun and come down and banged away at the deer. Baldy was a dead shot, but he didn't hit that deer. She went on back into the woods like nothing had bothered her at all. The next evening when he come down and fed his hogs, the same thing happened. The white deer come up out of the woods, hopped over into the pen and begun to eat the mash and slops away from the hogs. Baldy had brought his gun, this time loaded with buckshot. So he banged away pime blank at the deer. But he couldn't hit her. She went on back into the woods like nothing had happened.

"Well, Baldy was not to be outdone. So that night he got out a silver dollar and melted it down and made himself a silver bullet. So the next evening he was all prepared.

"He went down and fed his hogs and stood waiting with his gun all loaded with the silver bullet. Sure enough, up come the deer, snow white and beautiful as ever, out of the woods. She hopped over in the pen and begun to eat the way she had done before. Then it was Baldy let her have it full blast with his silver bullet.

"But bless your life, he hardly noticed whether he hit the deer or not. For right after he fired off his gun at the deer and she had plunged and hobbled away back into the woods, he heard the most outdacious yowling and screeching going on up at the house behind him. The children come running out on the porch hollering for him to hurry and see what had happened bad to Grandma.

"So he run up to the house and into the room and there lay Grandma on the floor writhing and twisting and screeching with pain. She had been shot clean through the leg and blood was pouring all out over the floor.

"Yes, sir, Grandma was a hag, that's what she was—a witch woman." (Paul Green)

The Cat

Once upon a time a black man was road-hustling down that lonesome road, and night came on. He stopped at a house to see if he could find a place to sleep. No, said the white man, he was too crowded, but down the road was a house he could stay in, except that it was haunted. The black fellow said he wasn't scared of anything.

He got to the old house, built a fire in the fireplace, roasted some sweet potatoes, and thought how lucky he was. As he went to sleep, raindrops spattered on the roof.

A little after midnight, he heard a sound and got up to see what it was. After looking around and finding nothing, he sat down before the fire and took off his shoes. Uh-huh, un-huh, uhhh. He felt a presence in the room. He twisted around and saw this terrible thing sitting on the box right beside him. It was all bones, no skin, just all bones. And then the thing rattled itself and grinned, and turned into a big black cat. It said in a meowing voice, "Seems like ain't nobody here but me and you tonight."

The black fellow said, "If I can just stand up a little bit, won't be nobody here but you." And with that, he yelled and jumped right through the window, and ran and ran till he dropped in the road.

He heard that awful meowing voice again. "That surely was some race we had." Race! That cat didn't know anything about racing and running. This time, that black man didn't run, he flew, flew right into the white man's house.

"You scared me about to death," said the white man. "What are you doing with that window sash hanging around your neck? Take it off." The black fellow did. "Are you going back to that haunted house to get your shoes?"

"No," said the black man, "I guess they can stay up there with about one hundred more pairs I saw by the fireplace."

Little Anse and the Carpenter

You'll find Mr. Joe John Collins's place up the winding hill road yonder, with fields terraced up slope, growing good-looking corn, and nice stock in Mr. Joe John's barns and pens, and he'd feed ary hungry neighbor, or tend ary sick one. All that sorrowed him, this day I mention, was his little boy Anse—crippled ever since he fell off the wagon and it run over both his legs.

That noon a stranger-man tramped into sight up the road's curve and stopped at Mr. Joe John's mail box. "Wonder if there might be a job of work for me," he said. "I'm a carpenter." And he showed the tool kit he carried.

Mr. Joe John liked the looks of the carpenter; so he said, "Yes. Come here across the yard. See that neighbor-house yonder?"

Between the two houses run a foot path, but midway across was dug a deep ditch, with water running down from above.

"Me and that neighbor-man was like two brothers once," said Mr. Joe John. "Then we fell out over a piece of land, and he dug that ditch to show he don't want me coming on his place. Now I'll go him one better. I want you to take these planks and poles and build me a board fence along this side the ditch, so he can't even see me over here."

The carpenter studied. Then he allowed, "I can do something you like."

"All right. Now I'm going to the upper field to chop weeds. See you later."

Mr. Joe John went, and the carpenter set to work. Like ary lone working man, he started in to sing. Not a silly song, nor purely a funny one, but you felt good to hear it, or, I reckon, to sing it. In Mr. Joe John's house, little Anse heard, and got off the couch and took his crutches and began to inch out there, on his poor swunk-up little legs. And when he got to where the carpenter was working, little Anse smiled and the carpenter smiled back at him.

All that day the carpenter worked and talked to little Anse, and when he finished he went back to the house, and there came Mr. Joe John. "All finished?" he asked the carpenter.

"Yes," the carpenter replied him; "come and see."

And Mr. Joe John went to look, and gentlemen! That carpenter hadn't build ary fence at all! He'd up and used that lumber to make a foot-bridge over the ditch, and across the bridge come walking the neighbor with his hand stuck out.

"Joe John," he said, "you don't know how dog-sorry I was I dug that ditch. But now you build this bridge, Joe John, to show you never favored us being cut off—"

Mr. Joe John shook his old friend's hand. "Why," he said, "I'm just as pleased as you are. But don't credit me with the bridge notion. This carpenter here, he thought it up."

They both looked round. The carpenter had hoisted up his tool kit, ready to leave. He smiled at them. Then, before he was gone, he put his free hand on little Anse's head, just half a second.

He said, "Throw away those crutches."

Little Anse flung them away. And fast as ary boy ever ran, he run to his daddy.

Next moment, the carpenter wasn't there. But all three of them knew who he was, and how he's with us always, the same as he promised, even to the end of the earth. (Manly Wade Wellman)

Girl at the Underpass

Not long ago, but before interstate highways ran around towns and cities, a young man left Greensboro late one night to drive to his home in Lexington. At that time, just east of Jamestown, the old road dipped through a tunnel under the train tracks. The young man knew the road well, but it was a thick foggy night in early summer and he drove cautiously, especially when he neared the Jamestown underpass. Many wrecks had taken place at that spot. He slowed down on the curve leading to the tunnel and was halfway through it when his eyes almost popped out of his head. Standing on the roadside just beyond the underpass was an indistinct white figure with arm raised in a gesture of distress. The young man quickly slammed on his brakes and came to a stop beside the figure.

It was a girl, young, beautiful, resplendent in a long white evening dress. Her troubled eyes were glaring straight toward him. Obviously she wás in need. He jumped from the car and ran around to where she stood motionless. "Can I help you?"

"Yes." Her voice was low, strange. "I want to go home. I live in High Point."

He opened the door, and she got in. As they drove off, he said, "I'm glad I came by. I didn't expect to find anyone like you on the road so late at night."

"I was at a dance." She spoke in a monotone. "My date and I had a quarrel. It was very bad. I made him drop me back there."

He tried to continue the conversation, but she would say nothing more until they were into High Point. "Turn at the next left," she said. "I live three doors on the right." He parked before a darkened house, got out of the car and went around to open the door for her. There was no one there! He looked into the back seat. No one! He thought she might have rushed up the sidewalk and out of sight.

Confused and undecided what to do next, he thought it only reasonable to find out if she had entered the house. He went up the steps and knocked on the door. No one came. He knocked again. There was no sound anywhere. After a third knock, through the side panes a dim light appeared from the pitch-black hallway. Finally the door was opened by a white-haired woman in a night robe.

"I brought a girl to this house," he explained, "but now I can't find her. Have you seen her? I picked her up out on the highway."

"Where?"

"At the Jamestown underpass. She told me she had been to a dance and was on her way home."

"Yes, I know," said the woman wearily. "That was my daughter. She was killed in a wreck at that tunnel five years ago tonight. And every year since, on this very night, she signals a young man like you to pick her up. She is still trying to get home."

The young man turned from the doorway, speechless. The dim light in the house went out. He drove on to Lexington, but never has he forgotten, nor will he ever forget, the beautiful hitchhiker and how she vanished into the night.

Old Buck at Rodanthe

Every January during the celebration of Old Christmas on the Outer Banks at Rodanthe, a terrible creature called Old Buck appears. He is there to punish children and is the very opposite of Santa Claus, who comes at Christmas to reward them. Since the real Old Buck has never been seen, the Old Buck at the celebration is merely his likeness. Even the little boys and girls know that the fearful animal is only two men under a cow's hide, holding horns and a bull's head in front of them.

The real Old Buck came to America long, long ago from Norway or Denmark. He took up residence in a pine forest down below Cape Hatteras and was known as "the wild bull of Trent Woods." Like the real Santa Claus, he never shows himself; but like the Santa Clauses whom we see in the stores at Christmas, the Old Buck at Rodanthe is a representation. He is not the monster himself.

The village of Rodanthe has two Christmases: the new one on December 25, and the old one on January 5. In 1752 when the English dropped eleven days in changing from the Julian to the Gregorian calendar, many old-timers said they would still cling to the old calendar, which they believed to be the "true" one. In time, they accepted the new date but would not abandon the old Christmas day that now came on January 5. Along the Outer Banks, children are lucky: they are visited by Santa Claus twice. Old Buck, however, comes only at Old Christmas.

After dancing and singing on the night of January 5 (or some Saturday near that date), the effigy of Old Buck enters the schoolhouse where the Rodanthe folks and their visitors are gathered. Shouts go up. A third man sits astride Old Buck and tells him to caper."Caper, Buck! Caper, Buck!" The demon dashes here and there about the room, and the boys and girls pretend to be afraid and draw back in their seats. Finally, the braver boys attack Old Buck with sticks, hoping they can defeat him and the evil he symbolizes. Just as it seems that Old Buck will be overcome by the boys, he makes his exit from the hall. Applause and cheers come from everyone present, for the Spirit of Christmas has been saved for another year.

It is said that once outside the schoolhouse, Old Buck becomes his real self. He races down the sandbanks to his hideaway among the pine trees in Trent Woods, and there he keeps out of sight for another twelve months.

Governor Bob Scott Tells about Governor Fowle's Ghost

There's a knock at the Executive Mansion and it isn't at the front door. It's not in the water pipes, either. While I don't believe in ghosts, someone speculated that it just might be Governor Fowle on the prowl in the spacious old building. Here's the story in a nutshell:

On the second floor of the Mansion, one of the bedrooms has traditionally been known as the Governor Fowle Bedroom. This is the bedroom used by the first occupant of the present Governor's Mansion, Governor Daniel G. Fowle, who moved into it in 1891.

In the Governor Fowle Bedroom, when I moved into the Mansion, there was a bed of very sturdy construction known as the Governor Fowle Bed. It was of the standard length of that day, but was extra wide. History tells us that this bed was made to order by Governor Fowle, a widower who often allowed his young son to come in and sleep with him. The young child thrashed around so much that Governor Fowle, being a large man himself, wanted more room and had the bed of extra width constructed.

Governor Fowle died during his term of office, and the story goes that he died in his large-sized bed and was found dead in the bed by his young son. So far as I know, the bed has remained in use at the Mansion during the ensuing years. I know that my predecessor, Governor Dan K. Moore, used the Governor Fowle Bed.

When our family moved into the Executive Mansion in January of 1969, I chose the Governor Fowle room as my bedroom because it was spacious, had a work desk, and was convenient to the upstairs study. I used the bed all during the year of 1969 and the early part of 1970. However, the bed was a little too short for me and my feet were constantly pressed up against the footboard. This caused me to sleep a little bit catty-cornered on the bed.

Recently, I was sitting at my desk working, gazing in the general direction of the bed. I became aware that the bed was not level. It appeared that each of the four corners stood at a different height from the floor. I got a yardstick from the kitchen and measured each corner height from the floor. I was correct in that no two corners were the same height. Therefore, the bed was obviously not level. This, with the discomfort of sleeping crossways on the bed, made me determined that I was going to get a new bed. I resolved to myself that I would not

spend the four years in the Executive Mansion in a bed as uncomfortable as that.

In discussing this with the First Lady, I strongly suggested that we purchase a king-size bed with no footboard from Craftique Furniture Company in Mebane, that we pay for this bed ourselves, and that when we left the Executive Mansion at the end of our term, we could take this new bed home to our farm with us. Mrs. Scott agreed to this, and our new bed was ordered. When it arrived, the Governor Fowle Bed was stored on the third floor of the Executive Mansion, where it is today.

One evening a few days later, Mrs. Scott and I were both in the bedroom reading (at approximately 10 P.M.), and we heard this rather strange knocking that appeared to be coming from within the wall near where the headboard of the Governor Fowle Bed had stood. The knocking lasted for at least one minute. The knocking had a rather unusual cadence to it, much like the bouncing of tennis balls after being dropped from a rather high distance. After the first knock, there was a long pause of several seconds. Then there was the second knock and a slightly less lengthy pause, then the third knock, and the pause following that was even less in length, until finally the pauses at the end were almost negligible.

Mrs. Scott and I paid no attention to the knock for the first several nights that it occurred. Then we began to notice that this knocking, which was not very loud, occurred every night. Further, it occurred around 10 o'clock, although there might be a variation of as much as thirty minutes. We discussed this several times, joked about ghosts in the house, then soon found ourselves listening for this knocking each night.

At first, we speculated that it might have some connection with the water pipes. However, there should not be any water pipes running in that particular section of the wall since it is not very close to the bathroom. Furthermore, we checked hurriedly when the knocking occurred to see if anyone was drawing water in the Mansion at that time. We were unable to find anyone drawing water when this knocking occurred. In addition to this fact, the knocking does not occur at other times when water is being drawn.

We, of course, do not believe in ghosts. However, the knocking does occur, and it is usually about the same time each night. For lack of a better explanation, we have named the knock the Governor Fowle Ghost. We assume that it is the ghost of Governor Fowle, requesting that the bed in which he died be replaced in the room.

There are two little sidelights to this story. One is that Mrs. Scott and I spent our honeymoon in this room and slept in the Governor Fowle Bed on September 1, 1951. [The narrator's father, W. Kerr Scott, was governor at that time.] The other is that the daughter of Governor Fowle today lives just down the street from the Executive Mansion. When a new governor moves into the Mansion, she soon thereafter pays a courtesy call on the new residents of the Executive Mansion. There are two questions she usually asks: "Is Father's portrait still hanging?" and "Is Father's bed still in his room?"

The bed isn't, but the knock is. (Robert W. Scott)

Notes and Sources

Legends usually are associated with specific events, places, or persons and extend some happening, or supposed happening, in remote or historic time with action either plausible or supernatural. To the legends in this collection have been unapologetically added a number of Indian myths and folk yarns not entirely unfamiliar. The three genres are literary cousins and get along very well with one another. Among the forty-eight selections are the best-known North Carolina legends, such as those about Blackbeard's last fight, the Brown Mountain lights, and Governor Fowle's ghost.

Ten of the legends, myths, and folk stories included here were found to have already an appropriate content, manner of telling, and length suitable for this collection. Furthermore, narrators like Adelaide L. Fries, Paul Green, Julia Montgomery Street, Manly Wade Wellman, F. Roy Johnson, Blackwell P. Robinson, and Governor Robert W. Scott are excellent storytellers, and their contributions provide diversity and distinction. To fit the allotted space, most of the selections had to be adapted from primary and/or secondary sources. Considering how legends are amplified from a mere detail into extended and even elaborate versions, primary sources most often are simply nonexistent.

North Carolina has been well served by dedicated writers eager to preserve our lore. Richard Benbury Creecy, Howard W. Odum, J. Mason Brewer, John Harden, Charles Harry Whedbee, Louise R. Booker, Horton Cooper, Fred T. Morgan, Nancy Roberts, and John Parris—in addition to some of those already mentioned—have written books popularizing and safeguarding our folk heritage. Throughout the years *State*, the Raleigh periodical, has been receptive to publicizing North Carolina legends, both the well known and the less familiar; and the *North Carolina Folklore Journal* (established in 1948) is a mine of documents exploring our commonly held beliefs.

LARGE TURTLE, by Charles Lanman, in *Letters from the Alleghany Mountains* (New York: G. P. Putnam, 1849), 63.

———

THE MOON-EYED PEOPLE, by Julia Montgomery Street, Winston-Salem. Based on a paragraph in Wilbur G. Zeigler and Ben S. Grosscup, *The Heart of the Alleghanies* (Raleigh: Alfred Williams, 1883), 16; and other sources.

———

JUDACULLA ROCK. Adapted from James Mooney, *Myths of the Cherokee* (Washington, D.C.: Bureau of American Ethnology, 1900), 337-341, 479-480; John Parris, *Mountain Bred* (Asheville: Citizen-Times Publishing Company, 1967), 216-217; and Julia Montgomery Street, *Judaculla's Handprint and Other Mysterious Tales from North Carolina* (Chapel Hill: Briarpatch Press, 1975), 23-25.

———

STARLIGHT AT BLOWING ROCK. Based on "Legend of Blowing Rock," undated, unidentified newspaper clipping, Brown Collection, Manuscript Division, Duke University Library. See also C. R. Sumner, "Indian Story Claims Upside-Down Breeze at Blowing Rock Created To Aid 2 Lovers," Asheville *Citizen-Times*, August 3, 1955; and Edward Garner, "Why Blowing Rock Blows," *State* (Raleigh), XXXV (June 15, 1967), 7. Romantic legends of lovelorn Indian braves or maidens plunging from a steep precipice have attached themselves to almost every popular mountain height in North Carolina.

———

WACCAMAW. For a portion of this myth, see the feature story on Lake Waccamaw by Jim Stingley, *News and Observer* (Raleigh), June 26, 1966.

Susan Schulken composed a poem based on the legend which appeared in the *Tar Heel Junior Historian*, XVII (Spring, 1978), 27-28. At the time, the author was a student at the Waccamaw Academy. Here is her poem:

THE LEGEND OF THE LAKE

Way long time ago lived an Indian princess
Whose home was a mound of flowers tall
This maiden was comely—a beauty was she—
And her name was Waccamaw.

She tended the garden and taught all the tribes
Of the lore of the Great Spirit Manitou.
So Manitou blessed her, guarded and kept her,
Shielded her heart from sorrow.

Now far to the north of this beautiful land
Lived the savage tribe of the black bear claw.
The prince of this tribe loved the pretty young maiden
Whose name was Waccamaw.

"O, dear Prince Ashbow, I shan't be your wife,
For by oath I am bound to Manitou.
I've pledged not to marry; this garden's my life.
Dear Ashbow, it must be so."

Her words sparked his anger and kindled his wrath.
He cursed the garden by the black bear claw.
His warriors then Ashbow led off to war
Against the tribe called Waccamaw.

The maiden saw the slaughter of her dear tribe
And prayed from her heart to Manitou,
"Dear Spirit, let me die now, and let my mound sink
Into a lake of waters low."

The sun, it descends on a lone sandbank—
'Tis the grave of the princess fair and small.
And where her mound once stood is a lake,
And its name is Waccamaw.

———

PRINCE MADOC THE WELSHMAN. For centuries the legendary voyages
and discoveries of Prince Madoc ab Owain Gwynedd have attracted
the attention of investigators. In 1805 Robert Southey, England's poet
laureate, popularized the subject in his long poem *Madoc*; its text in
The Complete Poetical Works of Robert Southey (New York: Appleton, 1850) is accompanied by extensive notes. Among the scholarly
summaries of documents and theories are those in Richard Deacon,
*Madoc and the Discovery of America: Some New Lights on an Old
Controversy* (London: Frederick Muller, 1967), and Samuel Eliot
Morison, *The European Discovery of America: The Northern
Voyages, A.D. 500-1600* (New York: Oxford University Press, 1971),
84-87.

VIRGINIA DARE THE WHITE DOE. Based on "The White Doe Chase: A Legend of Olden Times," a novelette by Raleigh writer Mary Ann Mason, native of New Bern, in the *Semi-Weekly Raleigh Register*, March 27, March 30, and April 3, 1861. At the end of the third installment, Mrs. Mason appended this note: "At her mother's knee in early childhood, the writer of this story heard the Legend of The White Doe Chase, which was believed by numbers of superstitious persons, at the period immediately preceding the Revolution; though with the Legend, was imparted no explanation; that has been supplied by the imagination of the writer." The novelette was reprinted in *Our Living and Our Dead* (Raleigh), III (December, 1875), 753-771, and later served as basis for the long narrative poem by Sallie Southall Cotten, *The White Doe: The Fate of Virginia Dare, an Indian Legend* (Philadelphia: J. B. Lippincott, 1901) and the shorter prose version "Legend of the White Doe" in Richard Benbury Creecy, *Grandfather's Tales of North Carolina History* (Raleigh: Edwards and Broughton, 1901), 15-18. The magical transformation of a girl into a deer comes from ancient Irish mythology (Stith Thompson, *Motif-Index*, D-114.1.1.1). For a similar story see, later in this book, "Paul Green Hears about the Harnett Hag."

BATTS GRAVE. Adapted from "Legend of Batz's Grave," in Richard Benbury Creecy, *Grandfather's Tales of North Carolina History* (Raleigh: Edwards and Broughton, 1901), 19-21, where the settler's name is given as Jesse Batz. See also William P. Cumming, *The Southeast in Early Maps* (Princeton, N.J.: Princeton University Press, 1958), 21-24; and William S. Powell, *The North Carolina Gazetteer* (Chapel Hill: University of North Carolina Press, 1968), 26.

THE SHIP OF FIRE. Based on "The Pirates and the Palatines: A Legend of North-Carolina," *Magnolia* (Charleston, S.C.), New Series, I (July, 1842), 32-34, reprinted in the *Carolina Watchman* (Salisbury), September 24, 1842. William Gilmore Simms later embellished the legend, without substantially altering the narrative line, as "The Ship of Fire," in *Southward Ho! A Spell of Sunshine* (New York: Redfield, 1854), 334-346. The *Magnolia* version was reprinted, with notes, in *North Carolina Folklore*, V (July, 1958), 23-26. See also the title story in Charles Harry Whedbee, *The Flaming Ship of Ocracoke & Other Tales of the Outer Banks* (Winston-Salem: John F. Blair, 1971), 13-20.

BLACKBEARD'S LAST FIGHT. The literature on Blackbeard is volu-minous, ranging from Captain Charles Johnson [Daniel Defoe], *A General History of Pyrates* (London: T. Warner, second edition, 1724) to Robert E. Lee, *Blackbeard the Pirate: A Reappraisal of His Life and Times* (Winston-Salem: John F. Blair, 1974).

THE BIRDS WEREN'T SINGING. See Malcolm Fowler, "The Day the Birds Quit Singing," *State* (Raleigh), VII (April 27, 1940), 8, 25; Malcolm Fowler, *They Passed This Way: A Personal Narrative of Harnett County History* ([Lillington]: Harnett County Centennial, Inc., 1955), 6-7; and William S. Powell, "Johnsonville," in *The North Carolina Gazetteer* (Chapel Hill: University of North Carolina Press, 1968), 255.

TROUBLES IN BATH TOWN. For the Whitefield story, see Blanche Marsh, "Preacher Who Put the Curse on Bath," *State* (Raleigh), XLV (July, 1977), 21, 56. The tale of the hoofprints is one of the most widely known legends in North Carolina, and its versions are numerous and diverse; see Bill Sharpe, "The Horse's Hoofprints," *State* (Raleigh), V (February 26, 1938), 5; [Leonard Rapport], "Magic Horse Tracks," in W. C. Hendricks (ed.), *Bundle of Troubles and Other Tarheel Tales* (Durham: Duke University Press, 1943), 172-177; "The Strange Hoof-Marks at Bath," in John Harden, *The Devil's Tramping Ground and Other North Carolina Mystery Stories* (Chapel Hill: University of North Carolina Press, 1949), 69-77; George E. Knox, "Riding His Horse to Hell," in *The Frank C. Brown Collection of North Carolina Folklore* (Durham: Duke University Press, 7 volumes, 1952-1964), I, 641-642; and "The Devil's Hoofprints," in Charles Harry Whedbee, *Legends of the Outer Banks and Tar Heel Tidewater* (Winston-Salem: John F. Blair, 1966), 92-99.

OLD DAN TUCKER. Adapted from the anonymous article in *State* (Raleigh), XVIII (April 28, 1951), 4, 40. The folk song, as apart from the legend, is treated in Henry M. Belden and Arthur Palmer Hudson (eds.), *Folk Songs from North Carolina* and volume III of *The Frank C. Brown Collection of North Carolina Folklore* (Durham: Duke University Press, 7 volumes, 1952-1964), 114-118. When Calvin Henderson Wiley's novel *Roanoke* was published in England, it was retitled *Adventures of Old Dan Tucker, and His Son Walter* (London:

Willoughby and Co., 1851). In it, Pocosin Dan Tucker, a renowned fiddler, is associated with Virginia's Old Zip Coon during Revolutionary times in eastern North Carolina.

_____

How Dan'l Boone Nearly Nipped a Romance, by an anonymous writer, in *North Carolina Folklore*, I (June, 1948), 5. Based on a legend collected by Furman Bishop, Denton, North Carolina.

_____

Betsy Dowdy's Ride. See accounts in Richard Benbury Creecy, *Grandfather's Tales of North Carolina History* (Raleigh: Edwards and Broughton, 1901), 90-95; and Blackwell Robinson (ed.), *The North Carolina Guide* (Chapel Hill: University of North Carolina Press, 1955), 304-305. Nell Wise Wechter's *Betsy Dowdy's Ride* (Winston-Salem: John F. Blair, 1960) is a novel for young readers.

_____

Mary Slocumb's Dream. For the source of this legend, see John H. Wheeler, *Historical Sketches of North Carolina, from 1584 to 1851* (Philadelphia: Lippincott, Grambo and Co., 2 volumes in 1, 1851), I, 457-460. John B. Flowers III questions the legend's credibility in "Did Polly Slocumb Ride to the Battle of Moore's Creek Bridge?" Lower Cape Fear Historical Society *Bulletin*, XIX (February, 1976).

_____

The Little Red Man, by Adelaide L. Fries, Winston-Salem, 1935. From *The Frank C. Brown Collection of North Carolina Folklore* (Durham: Duke University Press, 7 volumes, 1952-1964), I, 669-670.

_____

Old Quawk. See "Old Quork [sic]," in Charles Harry Whedbee, *Legends of the Outer Banks and Tar Heel Tidewater* (Winston-Salem: John F. Blair, 1966), 57-63; and "The New Career of Old Quawk," *State* (Raleigh), XLII (July, 1974), 48.

_____

The Devil's Tramping Ground. The best-known version of this popular tale is the title story in John Harden, *The Devil's Tramping Ground and Other North Carolina Mystery Stories* (Chapel Hill: University of North Carolina Press, 1949), 53-60.

YOUNG ANDREW JACKSON'S SKYLARKING. Based on Theresa Meroney Thomas, "How Jackson Broke Up a Dance," *State* (Raleigh), IV (January 23, 1937), 5, 16; and Horton Cooper, "The Ghost of Andrew Jackson," *News and Observer* (Raleigh), October 27, 1968.

PRESIDENT WASHINGTON AND BETSY BRANDON. Among the several accounts of this legend are Ada Viele, "Betsy Brandon's Guest," *State Normal Magazine* (Greensboro), XII (January, 1908), 117-118; and Richard Walser and Julia Montgomery Street, "Hoecake for Breakfast," *North Carolina Parade* (Chapel Hill: University of North Carolina Press, 1966), 62-68.

ROAN MOUNTAIN AND ITS MUSIC. See Charles Lanman, *Letters from the Alleghany Mountains* (New York: G. P. Putnam, 1849), 148; and John Parris, "Ghostly Choir of Roan Mountain," in *My Mountains, My People* (Asheville: Citizen-Times Publishing Company, 1957), 250-252.

AT CHIMNEY ROCK. See "Extraordinary Phenomenon," *Raleigh Register and North-Carolina State Gazette*, September 15, 1806; Wilbur G. Zeigler and Ben S. Grosscup, *The Heart of the Alleghanies* (Raleigh: Alfred Williams, 1883), 245-246; and *North Carolina Folklore*, IX (December, 1961), 23-26.

THE HONEYMOON. This is an old folk yarn. The version here is based on a retelling in John W. Moore, *The Heirs of St. Kilda: A Story of the Southern Past* (Raleigh: Edwards, Broughton and Co., 1881), 70-73.

THE PORTRAIT OF THEODOSIA BURR. Based on many accounts both historical and legendary. See, for example, B. A. Botkin (ed.), *A Treasury of Southern Folklore* (New York: Crown Publishers, 1949), 319-321; Charles Harry Whedbee, *Legends of the Outer Banks and Tar Heel Tidewater* (Winston-Salem: John F. Blair, 1966), 77-91; F. E. Winslow, "Letter Adds to History of Theodosia's Portrait," *News and Observer* (Raleigh), October 22, 1967; and Jonathan Daniels, "The Mysterious Theodosia," *News and Observer* (Raleigh), February 8, 1970.

A SPEECH FOR BUNCOMBE. See *City of Washington Gazette*, February 26, 1820, and W. D. [William Darlington], "Speaking for Bunkum," *Historical Magazine*, II (October, 1858), 311-312. See also Norman E. Eliason, *Tar Heel Talk* (Chapel Hill: University of North Carolina Press, 1956), 123, and Richard Walser (ed.), *The North Carolina Miscellany* (Chapel Hill: University of North Carolina Press, 1964), 150-151. The story has been told many times.

———

PETER STEWART NEY, SCHOOLMASTER. See LeGette Blythe's biography, *Marshall Ney: A Dual Life* (New York: Stackpole Sons, 1937); and George V. Taylor, "Scholarship and Legend: William Henry Hoyt's Research on the Ney Controversy," *South Atlantic Quarterly*, LIX (Summer, 1960), 360-396.

———

HOW NAGS HEAD GOT ITS NAME. The literature on Nags Head is extensive. See, for example, Bill Wright, "Making Tracks," *State* (Raleigh), XXXV (August 15, 1967), 16. Two early novels about the land pirates are Calvin Henderson Wiley's *Roanoke* (serialized, *Sartain's Union Magazine*, volumes IV-V, March-December, 1849) and Frank Vaughan's *Kate Weathers; or, Scattered by the Tempest* (Philadelphia: J. B. Lippincott and Company, 1878).

———

PETER DROMGOOLE. Based in part on Millie Johnson, "Legend of Dromgoole Duel Is Intriguing University Mystery," *Greensboro Daily News*, March 25, 1945. Kemp P. Battle, *History of the University of North Carolina* (Raleigh: Edwards and Broughton Printing Company, 2 volumes, 1907-1912), I, 343-344, calls it a "notable tradition."

———

LONG TIME BETWEEN DRINKS, by Blackwell Robinson, is from *The North Carolina Guide* (Chapel Hill: University of North Carolina Press, 1955), 470-471.

———

SPECTER AT THE GOLD MINE. Adapted from the much longer narrative by Nancy and Bruce Roberts, "The Haunted Gold Mine," in *This Haunted Land* (Charlotte: McNally and Loftin, 1970), 45-51. A comparable story of Gold Hill in Rowan County is "Ghost of the Old Mine," in Nancy Roberts, *An Illustrated Guide to Ghosts &*

Mysterious Occurrences in the Old North State (Charlotte: Heritage House, 1959), 43-46.

JESSE HOLMES THE FOOLKILLER. Based on extant Foolkiller letters in the *Milton Chronicle* between 1857 and 1879. See Durward T. Stokes (ed.), "Five Letters from Jesse Holmes, the Fool Killer, to the Editor of the *Milton Chronicle*," *North Carolina Historical Review*, L (Summer, 1973), 304-321; and Thomas C. Parramore, "Discovered: A Sixth Fool Killer Letter," *North Carolina Folklore Journal*, XXIII (August, 1975), 70-74.

SIREN OF THE FRENCH BROAD RIVER, by Charles M. Skinner, in *Myths & Legends of Our Own Land* (Philadelphia: J. B. Lippincott Company, 2 volumes, 1896), II, 77-78.

BROWN MOUNTAIN LIGHTS. Among the varied legends about these famous lights are those in *North Carolina Folklore*, I (June, 1948), 6-7, and *North Carolina Folklore Journal*, XX (February, 1972), 18-20.

THE WITCH BRIDE, by F. Roy Johnson, Murfreesboro, in *Witches and Demons in Folklore and History* (Murfreesboro: Johnson Publishing Company, 1969), 186. The informant was Mrs. Curtis Martin.

TAR HEELS. See Richard Walser, "How Did We Get To Be Tar Heels?" *News and Observer* (Raleigh), January 24, 1964.

THE EVIL HUNTER OF PURGATORY MOUNTAIN. Based on an article by Gray Johns (pseudonym), "What? Ghosts on Purgatory Mountain?" *State* (Raleigh), XLII (January, 1975), 13-15, 55.

TRAVELING CHURCH AT SWAN QUARTER. See Charles Harry Whedbee, *Legends of the Outer Banks and Tar Heel Tidewater* (Winston-Salem: John F. Blair, 1966), 100-105; and Dennis Rogers, "Church

Located on Lot by Storm, Hand of God," *News and Observer* (Raleigh), July 15, 1977.

———

Sop, Doll, Sop. See Isabel Gordon Carter, "Mountain White Folk-Lore: Tales from the Southern Blue Ridge," *Journal of American Folk-Lore*, XXXVIII (July-September, 1925), 354-355; and Richard Chase, *The Jack Tales* (Cambridge, Mass.: Houghton Mifflin Company, 1943), 76-82. In both accounts, the informant for this British-American folk tale was Mrs. Jane Gentry of Hot Springs, North Carolina, who had heard it and other Jack Tales "when she was a child from her grandfather who had learned them from his mother."

———

Maco Light. The story of lantern-swinging Joe Baldwin, undoubtedly one of the favorite North Carolina ghosts, has been told many times. See, for example, "The Ghosts at Maco Station," in John Harden, *Tar Heel Ghosts* (Chapel Hill: University of North Carolina Press, 1954), 44-51. A lengthy account of an investigation into the Maco specter by America's most famous ghost-hunter appears in Hans Holzer, *The Phantoms of Dixie* (Indianapolis and New York: Bobbs-Merrill Company, 1972), 69-90.

———

Mystery Ship of Diamond Shoals. Adapted from a more detailed account in David Stick, *Graveyard of the Atlantic* (Chapel Hill: University of North Carolina Press, 1952), 209-212.

———

Bladenboro's Vampire Beast. See Joseph F. Gallehugh, Jr., "The Vampire Beast of Bladenboro," *North Carolina Folklore Journal*, XXIV (August, 1976), 53-58, based on newspaper accounts, which are cited.

———

Paul Green Hears about the Harnett Hag, by Paul Green, Chapel Hill, in *North Carolina Folklore*, II (September, 1954), 13-14.

———

The Cat. Adapted from the dialect version in Howard W. Odum, *Cold Blue Moon: Black Ulysses Afar Off* (Indianapolis: Bobbs-Merrill, 1931), 26-27.

LITTLE ANSE AND THE CARPENTER, by Manly Wade Wellman, Chapel Hill, in *North Carolina Folklore*, III (July, 1955), 3-4, as narrated to him in 1951 by Ben Green of Bat Cave, North Carolina. In a somewhat different form, "On the Hills and Everywhere" repeats the story in Wellman's *Who Fears the Devil?* (Sauk City, Wis.: Arkham House, 1963), 180-190. Reprinted in this volume by permission of the author.

———

GIRL AT THE UNDERPASS. The Vanishing Hitchhiker has been seen in almost every part of the United States and, indeed, throughout the world. See Richard M. Dorson, *American Folklore* (Chicago: University of Chicago Press, 1959), 249-250, and Richard M. Dorson, *Buying the Wind* (Chicago: University of Chicago Press, 1964), 506-507. For her appearances in North Carolina, see "The Lovely Apparition," in Nancy Roberts, *An Illustrated Guide to Ghosts & Mysterious Occurrences in the Old North State* (Charlotte: Heritage House, 1959), 9-10, and Douglas J. McMillan, "The Vanishing Hitchhiker in Eastern North Carolina," *North Carolina Folklore*, XX (August, 1972), 123-128.

———

OLD BUCK AT RODANTHE. See Catherine D. Meekins, "Old Christmas at Rodanthe," *State* (Raleigh), IV (December 19, 1936), 1, 21; and Richard Walser, "Old Christmas at Rodanthe," *North Carolina Folklore*, X (July, 1962), 22-25.

———

GOVERNOR BOB SCOTT TELLS ABOUT GOVERNOR FOWLE'S GHOST, by Robert W. Scott, Haw River. "The Governor Fowle Ghost at the Executive Mansion," *North Carolina Folklore*, XVIII (November, 1970), 115-116.